"I had never read a book like this before. If someone who is, or if you are attempting to experience what God's Word teaches about want to read."

Daniel L. Akin, President, Southeastern Baptist Theological Seminary

"Born in a father's grief and marked with a pastor's wisdom, *Dark Clouds, Deep Mercy* teaches each of us and the church how to pray along the journey of loss and despair. Vroegop presents biblical guidelines for bringing honest complaint and bold petition before God and for choosing to steadfastly trust in the One whose mercies never end."

M. Daniel Carroll R., Blanchard Professor of Old Testament, Wheaton College

"Too often Christians feel the pressure to pretend the gospel diminishes pain, while others lament their pain void of biblical truth and hope. I have longed for years for a book to demonstrate a balance on this issue. *Dark Clouds, Deep Mercy* captures beautifully the unique and powerful grace of the gospel in Christian lament. The book is well written, winsome, and refreshingly transparent. I wept as I read it."

Brian Croft, Senior Pastor, Auburndale Baptist Church, Louisville; Founder, Practical Shepherding; Senior Fellow, Church Revitalization, The Southern Baptist Theological Seminary

"Lament is the language of exiles and aliens, of the suffering and downcast. But it is also the language of a people who know how the story ends. This book teaches us that pouring out our complaint to God is an act of faith and hope. In a world where sorrow has been politicized and death hidden away, let Mark Vroegop teach you the Christian language of lament that gives voice to our sadness and our desperate need for God."

Abigail Dodds, author, *(A)Typical Woman: Free, Whole, and Called in Christ*

"Until Christ returns or calls us home, lament will be our God-given language for finding faith to endure in a fallen world. This book will help the church become more fluent in the language of lament and thus more conversant with the God who has borne our griefs and carried our sorrows."

Collin Hansen, Editorial Director, The Gospel Coalition; coauthor, *A God-Sized Vision: Revival Stories That Stretch and Stir*

"When our lives encounter inevitable pain, we need perspective and power to survive and thrive through the weight of the burden. Vroegop masterfully converges his own testimony of anguish with rich insight into the nature and promises of our God, who weeps, grieves, and cares deeply for his children. This book will serve as a toolbox and treasure to your soul."

Daniel Henderson, President, Strategic Renewal International; author, *Transforming Prayer* and *Old Paths, New Power*

"This book gives real hope to those in deep valleys. Vroegop challenges us to speak up through tears and tell God what hurts in a raw and real way that results in even deeper reverence. I recommend this book to everyone who wants to hope against hope in a God who listens even when we complain, who answers even when we doubt."

Garrett Higbee, Director of Pastoral Care, Great Commission Collective

"Lament is not just tears or pain in our own soul; lament is inviting Christ to come alongside our casket of loss. Lament is not just a prayer; it is a prayer expressing our pain in our fallen world. Lament does not stop at pain; through Christ's comforting presence, lament enriches our trust in our Father of compassion. Anyone who wants to learn biblically *and* experientially how to candidly call out to our comforting Father would benefit greatly from this book."

Robert W. Kellemen, Vice President of Strategic Development and Academic Dean, Faith Bible Seminary; author, *God's Healing for Life's Losses* and *Grief: Walking with Jesus*

"Profound. Tender. Strengthening. Crucial. Wise. This book helped me see something that's basic to Christianity that I hadn't fully grasped as basic. I began rereading it with my wife before finishing it the first time. Every pastor, counselor—and indeed, every Christian—should read it."

Jonathan Leeman, Editorial Director, 9Marks; author, *The Rule of Love*

"Mark Vroegop reminds us that grief and sorrow are not the denial of God's presence or a lack of faith in God's sovereign care. God calls us to lament, to give expression to our pain and sorrow, which in turn leads to authentic hope, healing, and health. Vroegop shepherds our hearts and shows us the path to discovering 'deep mercy in dark clouds.' This book is a hope-filled treasure!"

Crawford W. Loritts Jr., Senior Pastor, Fellowship Bible Church, Roswell, Georgia; author, *Unshaken*; Host, *Living a Legacy*

"This book shouts to us from the Psalms and Lamentations: *It's okay to cry, to grieve, to wonder why, and to come to God with our doubts and fears. Our heavenly Father can handle it. And in the end, he shows us grace and mercy.* This book is a wonderful antidote to the feel-good, happy, and superficial platitudes of so much of modern evangelicalism."

Erwin W. Lutzer, Pastor Emeritus, The Moody Church, Chicago

"There were seasons in my life when I really needed this book but did not have it. So I have read it now with both delight and regret: delight that it is finally here and regret that it was not here sooner. I have found myself saying, 'I wish I had known that,' or 'I wish I had done that.' The sooner you read this book, the less you will say those things to yourself!"

Jason C. Meyer, Pastor for Preaching and Vision, Bethlehem Baptist Church, Minneapolis

"Mark Vroegop winsomely introduces us to the lost art of lament. From the outside, the world of lament looks dark and foreboding, but as you enter it, light will shine on your soul in startling ways."

Paul E. Miller, Executive Director, seeJesus; author, *A Praying Life* and *J-Curve*

"Mark Vroegop has written a book that is a gift to the church—both to the one suffering and to the one who wants to help the sufferer. Through his own personal loss and practice of lament, he helpfully guides us in lament, showing us that to lament is Christian and to lament is to find hope even in the greatest pain."

Courtney Reissig, author, *Glory in the Ordinary*

"Vroegop's message is forged out of his personal journey, which validates the high value of healing through lament. But more importantly, he takes us to key passages of Scripture that assure us that God welcomes our agonizing cries of complaint as a step toward his grace and strength in our time of need."

Joseph M. Stowell, President, Cornerstone University; author, *The Upside of Down* and *Redefining Leadership*

"This book is born out of personal tragedy and loss. It is a gold mine of help for those who have suffered deep wounds from loss. Mark Vroegop masterfully blends his personal life, pastoral experience, and biblical exposition into a volume that shows how God's grace in lament and the cry of the heart in prayer teach you to trust God's purposes."

John D. Street, Chair, Graduate Department in Biblical Counseling, The Master's University and Seminary; President, Association of Certified Biblical Counselors

"If you allow it, this book will draw tears, unveil smiles, heal old wounds, increase your biblical understanding, and bring peace. Mark Vroegop gracefully points the way to the biblical light of mercy and hope amid misery and despair. Your pain can become a platform for helping others rather than a pit of self-pity, and this book will help you arrive at that better destination."

Thomas White, President, Cedarville University

"I am intensely grateful for *Dark Clouds, Deep Mercy* and would place it among the most important and influential books I've read in the past few years. If you are going through hard times, this book may provide more insight and comfort than any other book except for the Bible. If you are in ministry, please allow Vroegop to help you discover how 'the grace of lament' can serve the many hurting people in your congregation."

Donald S. Whitney, Professor of Biblical Spirituality and Associate Dean, The Southern Baptist Theological Seminary; author, *Spiritual Disciplines for the Christian Life* and *Praying the Bible*

"God has lovingly immersed one of his outstanding Bible expositors into the depths of human sorrow so that the rest of us can learn from him the important grace of lament. Through the tragic loss of his daughter, Mark has reflected deeply, studied the Bible carefully, and written beautifully to help us all walk more closely with our Savior."

Sandy Willson, Interim Senior Pastor, Covenant Presbyterian Church, Birmingham, Alabama

"I have watched as Mark Vroegop and his wife have navigated the difficult journey of loss, and I have witnessed in their lives the sweet fruit of godly lament. Vroegop provides a hope-filled guide to experiencing the mercy of God in the darkest nights, through the vital, healing grace of lament."

Nancy DeMoss Wolgemuth, author, *Adorned*; Teacher and Host, *Revive Our Hearts*

DARK CLOUDS, DEEP MERCY

Discovering the Grace of Lament

Mark Vroegop

Foreword by Joni Eareckson Tada

WHEATON, ILLINOIS

Published in association with the literary agency of Wolgemuth & Associates, Inc.

Cover design: Jeff Miller, Faceout Studios

First printing 2019

Printed in the United States of America

Trade paperback ISBN: 978-1-4335-6148-1
ePub ISBN: 978-1-4335-6151-1
PDF ISBN: 978-1-4335-6149-8
Mobipocket ISBN: 978-1-4335-6150-4

Library of Congress Cataloging-in-Publication Data

Names: Vroegop, Mark, 1971– author.

Title: Dark clouds, deep mercy: discovering the grace of lament / Mark Vroegop; foreword by Joni Eareckson Tada.

Description: Wheaton, Illinois: Crossway, [2019] | Includes bibliographical references and index.

Identifiers: LCCN 2018034125 (print) | LCCN 2018052571 (ebook) | ISBN 9781433561498 (pdf) | ISBN 9781433561504 (mobi) | ISBN 9781433561511 (epub) | ISBN 9781433561481 (trade paperback)

Subjects: LCSH: Laments in the Bible. | Bible. Psalms—Criticism, interpretation, etc. | Bible. Lamentations—Criticism, interpretation, etc. | Grief—Religious aspects—Christianity. | Suffering—Religious aspects—Christianity.

Classification: LCC BS1199.L27 (ebook) | LCC BS1199.L27 V76 2019 (print) | DDC 220.6/6—dc23

LC record available at https://lccn.loc.gov/2018034125

Crossway is a publishing ministry of Good News Publishers.

BP		32	31	30	29	28	27	26	25	24	23
19	18	17	16	15	14	13	12	11	10	9	8

To my wife, Sarah,
who courageously walked with me
through our pilgrimage of lament.
I love you.

To my daughter, Sylvia,
whom God used to teach me that
hard is hard; hard is not bad.
We miss you.

Contents

Foreword

When a broken neck ambushed my life and left me a quadriplegic, I felt as though God had smashed me underfoot like a cigarette. At night, I would thrash my head on the pillow, hoping to break my neck at a higher level and thereby end my misery. After I left the hospital, I refused to get out of bed; I told my sister, "Just close the drapes, turn out the light, and shut the door." My paralysis was permanent, and inside, I died.

You don't have to be in a wheelchair to identify. You already know that sad situations sometimes don't get better. Problems don't always get solved. Conflicts don't get fixed. Children die, couples divorce, and untimely deaths rock our world and shake our faith.

We try to manage, like jugglers spinning plates on long sticks. When we feel utterly overwhelmed, we try soaking in the tub, sweating on the treadmill, splurging on a new dress, or heading to the mountains for the weekend. We smile and say we are trusting God, but down deep we know it's a lie. We're only trusting that he doesn't load us up with more plates.

That's how I felt. But after weeks in bed, I got tired of being depressed, and I finally cried out, "God, if I can't die, *please* show me how to live." It was just the prayer God was waiting for.

From then on, I would ask my sister to get me up and park me in my wheelchair in front of my Bible. Holding a mouth stick, I would flip this way and that, looking for answers—*any* answer. I sought the help of a Christian counselor-friend who took me directly to the book of Lamentations. He showed me the third chapter:

> I am the man who has seen affliction . . .
> surely against me [God] turns his hand
>   again and again the whole day long. (Lam. 3:1, 3)

I marveled, thinking, *that's me!*

I was amazed to learn that God welcomes our laments. I would eventually learn—mainly through Lamentations and Psalms—that nothing is more freeing than knowing God understands. When we are in pain, God feels the sting in his chest. Our frustrations and questions do not fluster him. He knows all about them. He wrote the book on them. More astoundingly, he invites us to come and air our grievances before him.

And for moving through pain and grief, *Dark Clouds, Deep Mercy* is the *best* of guides. Mark Vroegop knows how to write on the subject: he's not only experienced deep suffering; he's pastored hurting people for over two decades. He shows the reader what to do with anger and depression—not sweep it under the carpet of your conscience or minimize it, but actually *do* something good with it.

If your plates are spinning out of control—if you are crying, "God, I can't live this way"—then please know that you have a companion in Mark Vroegop. Make his remarkable book your friend on this journey. Its gifted author has lived in the inner sanctum of Christ's suffering and is a faithful sage when it comes to finding practical help in the midst of pain. Let Mark guide you; let God's Spirit guide you—for hope is about to break on your horizon over the next few chapters.

Joni Eareckson Tada
Joni and Friends International Disability Center

Acknowledgments

I've wanted to write this book for over a decade. Without the support and encouragement of a host of people, it would never have become a reality.

I'm grateful for the people in two churches who were vital to my journey in lament. Calvary Baptist Church in Holland, Michigan, not only gave me the gift of serving as senior pastor from 1996 to 2008. They also cared for my family following the death of Sylvia, our daughter—even sending our family away for two weeks so we could begin the long process of healing. Our family will never forget their kindness to us when the dark clouds of unspeakable grief rolled in.

For the last ten years I've been privileged to lead the people of College Park Church in Indianapolis. Our journey through Job, Psalms, and Lamentations provided a working laboratory for every part of this book. These gracious and hungry people have devoured the Word and put it into practice in a way that continues to bring me great joy.

The elders of College Park Church graciously provided a sabbatical in 2014, when the vision for this book was birthed. Developing my skills as a writer was an objective, and Ann Kroeker became my writing coach. She was the first person to convince me not only that a book about lament was needed but also that I should write it. Her relentless encouragement and professional advice fueled the early development of this book.

Robert and Austin from Wolgemuth and Associates took a risk on an unpublished author. Their support was invaluable. They opened doors and provided guidance along each step of this journey. Without the two of them, this book would still just be a crazy idea.

Dave DeWit from Crossway offered thoughtful coaching in the early stages of the development of the manuscript. To have a man with such skill and compassion read my messy prose was one of the many grace gifts of this process. Dave's gift of encouragement kept my self-doubts at bay.

A team of friends made my manuscript better. Tim Whitney, Dale Shaw, Debbie Armbruster, Dustin Crowe, Dennis Swender, and Jackie Halderman all provided helpful critiques and suggestions. Their input and feedback were fuel for my soul as real people engaged with my thoughts.

I'm grateful to my wife, Sarah, who has been my companion on the path of lament for over twenty-five years. I've watched her live what I write about. A mother's grief is uniquely painful, and yet she kept lamenting and trusting—never giving in to despair. I've watched her lament with more grieving mothers than I can count. I've seen mercy emerge within dark clouds as pain became a platform, not a pit.

Finally, I'm grateful for a Savior who set his affection on me and set me free from the bondage of my sin. His crucifixion and resurrection remind me that he bought the right to make everything right. I long for the day when a little grave in Graafschap Cemetery will yield the body of my daughter, and my faith will be sight.

While I expectantly wait, I lament.

Introduction

Life in a Minor Key

A Personal Journey

The LORD gave, and the LORD has taken
away; blessed be the name of the LORD.
Job 1:21

Learning to lament began on my knees.

"No, Lord!" I pleaded. "Please not this!" It was 2004, and my wife, Sarah, awakened me, concerned that something was wrong with her pregnancy. A few days from her due date, she had not slept most of the night, waiting for our in-utero baby to move. Hours of tapping her tummy, shifting positions, and offering tear-filled prayers only increased my wife's concern. Inside her womb, stillness.

I cried out in prayer next to our bed.

Pregnancy was not new for us. Eight years earlier we were shocked to hear the word "twins" from an ultrasound technician.

Sarah carried our boys to thirty-nine weeks, nearly breaking the doctor's office record for the largest womb they'd seen for twins. Three days after delivery we carried our healthy kids home. And then, three years later, we were blessed with another son. In the four years of our marriage, we welcomed three healthy children into our lives.

Not everything in life was a breeze. We faced challenges. When our three children were born, I was the teaching pastor of a church in West Michigan. The demands on me as a young pastor were heavy. I was inexperienced, and the church never lacked for challenges. So we faced many struggles; life wasn't problem-free. However, my spontaneous prayer expressed a new depth of desperation.

I was frightened.

Later, that afternoon our doctor placed a monitor on Sarah's womb, searching for a heartbeat. Seconds passed. Multiple angles. Silence. I saw a concerned look form on his face. He suggested we move into the ultrasound room to determine what was happening. My wife's head dropped. She knew.

A few minutes later we could see our baby's body on the screen. I watched as our doctor navigated the small wand. I'd seen enough ultrasounds to know what he was looking for: the grainy flutter of a beating heart. Sarah was silent. The doctor pointed to the screen. "I'm so sorry," he said, "but the heart's not beating."

Our baby, only a few days from entering our lives, had died.

Sorrows Like Sea Billows

The crashing waves of grief in that moment were overwhelming. But our journey was only beginning. A few hours later we checked into the hospital. I sat by my wife's bed as she endured hours of labor. We prayed and cried together. About twenty-four hours after hearing the crushing news, I held the nine-pound body of my lifeless daughter, Sylvia. As I cradled her, swaddled in a hospital blanket, I longed for her to wake up. Her fully developed body looked so normal. But there was no breathing.

She was beautiful but not alive.

I felt such piercing grief and sorrow, it's impossible to fully describe. Pain and fear mingled together in a jumbled torrent of emotion. Thoughts about the future raced through my mind. Questions haunted me: How would my boys respond to this level of sadness? Would my wife ever be happy again? What if we never conceived another child? How could I live with this pain while feeling the need to have it all together as I pastored a church? Would our marriage make it?

So many questions.

So much fear.

Discovering Lament

Following Sylvia's death, I poured out my heart to the Lord with desperate candor. I fought the temptation to be angry with God. I wrestled with sadness that bored a hole in my chest. In the midst of my pain, I began to find words and phrases in the Bible that captured the emotions of my heart. Some leapt off the pages.

The Bible gave voice to my pain. Particular psalms became my own. I read these passages before, but I had never seen them or heard them like this. A years-long journey began. In that process, I discovered a minor-key language for my suffering: lament.

Although I had been a student of the Bible for many years, biblical lament was new for me. I didn't even know what to call it at the time. I was merely trying to voice my fears and struggles while at the same time pointing my heart toward God.

My quest for spiritual survival opened my heart to this historic and biblical form of prayer.

Sorrow tuned my heart to hear the song of lament.

The gut-level honesty expressed in lament was refreshing and helpful. You see, I knew the assurances of God's love in passages like Romans 8 and others. I believed somehow God would work out everything for his good purposes. I never doubted that.

Yet my grief was not tame.

It was vicious.

I battled fears, disappointments, and sorrow. And in my journey, I discovered the grace of lament, a song I never wanted to sing. However, once I was in the crucible, I was deeply thankful for this uninvited dimension of the Christian life.

Looking back, I can see how lament became my guide, my teacher, and my solace.

The years that followed Sylvia's death were a roller coaster of emotions and challenges. We suffered multiple miscarriages and a false-positive pregnancy. However, our painful yet honest prayers helped turn our agony into a platform for worship.

Lament helped us navigate the wilderness of our grief.

Uncomfortable with Lament

However, in that journey we also learned that many Christians, like us, were unfamiliar—even uncomfortable—with lament. When occasionally I candidly shared a few of the struggles of my soul, some people reacted with visible discomfort. Others quickly moved to a desperate desire to "find the bright side," a quick change of the subject, an awkward silence, or even physically excusing themselves to escape the tension.

When people stayed in the conversation, they often responded in unhelpful ways. In moments of attempted comfort, people said things like "I'm sure the Lord will give you another baby," "Maybe more people will come to faith because of the death of your daughter," or "The Lord must know he can trust you with this."

Every person meant well. I appreciated their attempts to address our pain. But it became clear that most people did not know how to join us in our grief.

Lament was just not familiar terrain.

Lament as Grace

As I read books on grief, I discovered many attempts to explain the purpose of pain or to walk readers through the stages of grief. While these are helpful at some level, they frequently missed or ignored the concept of lament. Finding an explanation or a quick solution for grief, while an admirable goal, can circumvent the opportunity afforded in lament—to give a person permission to wrestle with sorrow instead of rushing to end it. Walking through sorrow without understanding and embracing the God-given song of lament can stunt the grieving process.

I came to see lament as a helpful gift from the Lord.

Through this journey, I came to love Psalm 13. I had read it many times before. This time it was personal. It expressed my heart and served as a path for my grief. It kept my soul out of the ditches of despair and denial. I memorized the words. It became a help to my soul and to others in pain.

> How long, O LORD? Will you forget me forever?
>   How long will you hide your face from me?
> How long must I take counsel in my soul
>   and have sorrow in my heart all the day?
> How long shall my enemy be exalted over me?
>
> Consider and answer me, O LORD my God;
>   light up my eyes, lest I sleep the sleep of death,

lest my enemy say, "I have prevailed over him,"
  lest my foes rejoice because I am shaken.

But I have trusted in your steadfast love;
  my heart shall rejoice in your salvation.
I will sing to the LORD,
  because he has dealt bountifully with me. (vv. 1–6)

Through this personal odyssey, I began to see the redemptive value of lament and wonder why it was often missing. For example, I listened differently at funerals, and they seemed lament-lite. The absence of lament in our worship services also struck me. I noticed how the majority of songs were celebratory and triumphant. While I have nothing against celebration and pointing people toward hope, the depth of my grief caused me to long for the honest and candid spiritual struggle with pain. Celebration is certainly not wrong, but with a consistent absence of lament, it felt incomplete.

Through the years I began to talk about lament. I incorporated it into funeral services. I taught on it in my sermons. The effect was startling. Grieving people came out of the shadows. My life and pastoral ministry involved numerous conversations with hurting people. I began helping people discover how lament invites us to grieve and trust, to struggle and believe. I walked people through their grief by leading them—even encouraging them—to lament. I started to understand at a new level why the Psalms are so helpful to hurting people.

I began to see lament as a rich but untapped reservoir of God's grace.

Deep Mercy in Dark Clouds

The aim of this book is to help you discover the grace of lament—to encourage you to find deep mercy in dark clouds. The title is taken from two verses in Lamentations that seem to be a paradox. But they aren't.

> How the Lord in his anger
>> has set the daughter of Zion under a cloud! (Lam. 2:1)

> The steadfast love of the LORD never ceases;
>> his mercies never come to an end. (Lam. 3:22)

When the circumstances of life create dark clouds, I hope you'll come to embrace lament as a divinely given liturgy leading you to mercy. This historic song gives you permission to vocalize your pain as it moves you toward God-centered worship and trust. Lament is how you live between the poles of a hard life and trusting in God's sovereignty.

Lament is how we bring our sorrow to God. Without lament we won't know how to process pain. Silence, bitterness, and even anger can dominate our spiritual lives instead. Without lament we won't know how to help people walking through sorrow. Instead, we'll offer trite solutions, unhelpful comments, or impatient responses. What's more, without this sacred song of sorrow, we'll miss the lessons historic laments are intended to teach us.

Lament is how Christians grieve. It is how to help hurting people. Lament is how we learn important truths about God and our world. My personal and pastoral experience has convinced me that biblical lament is not only a gift but also a neglected dimension of the Christian life for many twenty-first-century Christians.

A broken world and an increasingly hostile culture make contemporary Christianity unbalanced and limited in the hope we offer if we neglect this minor-key song. We need to recover the ancient practice of lament and the grace that comes through it. Christianity suffers when lament is missing.

A Journey in Lament

This book charts a course for our journey. It will take us through an exploration of four lament psalms and the one biblical book dedicated to the subject: Lamentations. In part 1, I'll try to help you learn *to* lament. In part 2, I hope to show you what we learn *from* lament. And finally, in part 3, we'll explore how to live *with* lament—both personally and with others.

Although I didn't realize it at the time, Sylvia's stillbirth would be the beginning of my discovery of lament. The path of grief created an affection for the biblical language of sorrow that would extend into other areas of my life and pastoral ministry.

My fearful prayer—"Please not this!"—was only the beginning of a providential journey of learning to love lament and the grace that comes through it. Regardless of the circumstances in your life, this minor-key song can help you.

Join me on this journey.

There is deep mercy under dark clouds when we discover the grace of lament.

Reflection Questions

1. What is your story with pain or sorrow? What painful events in your life have shaped your soul and your understanding of God?
2. What are some of the questions and struggles you frequently have to fight when you are dealing with pain?
3. What are some of your favorite passages in the Bible that bring comfort and assurance to those who are suffering?
4. How would you define lament, and what is your perspective on it?
5. When you've had to help a friend or a loved one through the pain of suffering, what are some things you've found helpful and unhelpful?

PART 1

LEARNING TO LAMENT

PSALMS OF LAMENT

1

Keep Turning to Prayer

Psalm 77

In the day of my trouble I seek the Lord;
    in the night my hand is stretched out without wearying;
    my soul refuses to be comforted.
When I remember God, I moan.
Psalm 77:2–3

Who taught you to cry? The answer, of course, is "no one." Although you don't remember it, the first sound you made when you left the warm and protected home of your mother's womb was a loud wail.[1] A heartfelt protest.

Every human being has the same opening story. Life begins with tears. It's simply a part of what it means to be human—to cry is human.

---

1. I'm grateful for this concept as found in Michael Card, *A Sacred Sorrow: Reaching Out to God in the Lost Language of Lament* (Colorado Springs: NavPress, 2005), 19.

But lament is different. The practice of lament—the kind that is biblical, honest, and redemptive—is not as natural for us, because every lament is a prayer. A statement of faith. Lament is the honest cry of a hurting heart wrestling with the paradox of pain and the promise of God's goodness.

To Lament Is Christian

Belief in God's mercy, redemption, and sovereignty create lament. Without hope in God's deliverance and the conviction that he is all-powerful, there would be no reason to lament when pain invaded our lives. Todd Billings, in his book *Rejoicing in Lament*, helps us understand this foundational point: "It is precisely out of trust that God is sovereign that the psalmist repeatedly brings laments and petitions to the Lord. . . . If the psalmists had already decided the verdict—that God is indeed unfaithful—they would not continue to offer their complaint."[2] Therefore, lament is rooted in what we believe. It is a prayer loaded with theology. Christians affirm that the world is broken, God is powerful, and he will be faithful. Therefore, lament stands in the gap between pain and promise.

To cry is human, but to lament is Christian.

A few years ago I was leading a prayer meeting for our church staff. I placed an empty chair in a circle of other chairs. While we were singing, praying, and spontaneously reading Scripture, I invited people to make their way to the middle chair and offer a prayer of lament to the Lord. We'd been studying the subject as a church. I thought it would be good to put this minor-key song into practice. I also knew there was a lot of pain in the room.

After a few minutes of awkward silence, a brave young woman nervously moved to the middle chair. She clutched a

---

2. Todd Billings, *Rejoicing in Lament: Wrestling with Incurable Cancer and Life in Christ* (Grand Rapids, MI: Brazos, 2015), 58–59.

small card and sighed. Painful emotions were just under the surface. Her husband, who also served on our staff, quickly joined
and knelt beside her. Others soon followed, placing hands on
their shoulders—a simple but touching demonstration of entering their grief. With a trembling voice she read her lament:

> How long, O Lord? Will you forget me forever? How long will
> you withhold the blessing of a child from us? How long will we
> cry to you—how many more days, months, or years will pass
> with our arms remaining empty? How much longer will we
> struggle to rejoice with those who rejoice while we sit weeping?
> But I have trusted in your steadfast love. My heart shall rejoice
> in your salvation. I will sing to the Lord, because he has dealt
> bountifully with me! Thank you, Father![3]

In one short prayer she vocalized her deep sorrow while simul-
taneously reaffirming her trust. She wept and remembered. She
sobbed and trusted. She lamented.

After she prayed, another staff member made his way to the
same chair. "Here I am again, Lord! I don't like this chair, but
I know I need to come. My wife and I long for another baby to
adopt, and we are so tired of waiting and the emotional roller
coaster. But we are trusting."[4] By the time the prayer summit
was over, four couples mourned empty cribs. Lament provided
a language that anchored these grieving couples to what they
knew to be true while they waited.

One reason I have written this book is my love for people who
know the unwelcomed presence of pain. As a follower of Jesus,
I have personally walked through my own trauma of unexplain-
able loss and wrestled with troubling questions. As a pastor, I've
wept with countless people in some of the darkest moments of life.

---

3. From a former staff member of our church, who prefers to remain anonymous
(2016). Used by permission.
4. From a staff member, who prefers to remain anonymous (2016). Used by permission.

Every Christian experiences some kind of suffering and hardship. And I've seen the difference between those who learn to lament and those who don't. I've observed the way lament provides a critical ballast for the soul. No one seeks out the pain that leads to lament, but when life falls apart, this minor-key song is life-giving.

What Is Lament?

Before we start our journey exploring four psalms and the book of Lamentations, we need to define lament. Allow me to give you a brief overview, and then we'll see what it looks like in Psalm 77.

Lament can be defined as a loud cry, a howl, or a passionate expression of grief. However, in the Bible lament is more than sorrow or talking about sadness. It is more than walking through the stages of grief.

Lament is a prayer in pain that leads to trust.

Throughout the Scriptures, lament gives voice to the strong emotions that believers feel because of suffering. It wrestles with the struggles that surface. Lament typically asks at least two questions: (1) "Where are you, God?" (2) "If you love me, why is this happening?"[5] Sometimes these questions are asked by individuals. At other times they are asked by entire communities. Sometimes laments reflect upon difficult circumstances in general, sometimes because of what others have done, and sometimes because of the sinful choices of God's people in particular.

You might think lament is the opposite of praise. It isn't. Instead, lament is a path to praise as we are led through our brokenness and disappointment.[6] The space between brokenness and God's mercy is where this song is sung. Think of lament as the transition between pain and promise.

It is the path from heartbreak to hope.

---

5. Card, *Sacred Sorrow*, 17.
6. Card, *Sacred Sorrow*, 21.

The Pattern of Lament

Most biblical laments follow a pattern as God takes grieving people on a journey. This poetic odyssey usually includes four key elements: (1) an address to God, (2) a complaint, (3) a request, and (4) an expression of trust and/or praise.[7] For the purposes in this book, I'll use four words to help us learn to lament: *turn, complain, ask,* and *trust.* Part 1 explores these steps, helping us to know what they are and how to put them into practice.

Each step of lament is a part of a pathway toward hope. In the address, the heart is turned to God in prayer. Complaint clearly and bluntly lays out the reasons behind the sorrow. From there, the lamenter usually makes a request for God to act—to do something. Finally, nearly every lament ends with renewed trust and praise.

In this first chapter we will see how lament begins by turning to God in prayer. We'll discover the supply of grace that comes as we take the step of faith to reach out to God. Lament invites us to turn our gaze from the rubble of life to the Redeemer of every hurt. It calls us to turn toward promise while still in pain.

The Psalms are where our journey begins.

Psalms of Lament

The book of Psalms is filled with lament. No doubt that's why it is a cherished portion of Scripture. Aren't the Psalms one of the first places you turn to when you're in pain? The Psalms were the songbook for God's covenant community. They reflect the joys, struggles, sorrows, and triumphs of life. It's noteworthy that at least a third of the 150 psalms are laments. It is

---

7. Stacey Gleddiesmith, "My God, My God, Why? Understanding the Lament Psalms," *Reformed Worship*, June 2010, www.reformedworship.org/article /june-2010/my-god-my-god-why.

the largest category in the entire Psalter.[8] Whether the lament is corporate, individual, repentance-oriented, or imprecatory (strongly expressing a desire for justice), you cannot read the Psalms without encountering laments.

One out of three psalms is in a minor key. Just think about that! A third of the official songbook of Israel wrestles with pain. But consider how infrequently laments appear in our hymnals or in our contemporary songs. I find this curious and concerning. Could it be that our prosperity, comfort, and love of triumphalism are reflected in what we sing? Is it possible that our unfamiliarity with lament is a by-product of a subtle misunderstanding of Christian suffering? Don't get me wrong, there certainly is a place for celebration and joyful affirmation of the truths we believe. But I wonder about the long-term effect if the contemporary church and its people consistently miss this vital dimension of Christianity. The number of laments, their use, and their message invite us to consider the value of this biblical song of sorrow.

Laments are in the Bible for a reason.

When you put all this together, it's clear that this minor-key song is vital to the life of God's people. There's something uniquely Christian about lament, something redemptive, and something full of faith. I hope this book helps you to discover the grace of lament.

With this background, let's learn to lament by looking at the first element: turning our hearts to prayer.

Psalm 77: Keep Praying

I've chosen to start with Psalm 77 because it provides a wonderful example of the connection between lament and turning to God. It shows the beauty of pushing the heart toward God in

---

8. Bruce K. Waltke, James M. Houston, and Erika Moore, *The Psalms as Christian Lament: A Historical Commentary* (Grand Rapids, MI: Eerdmans, 2014), 1.

our pain. This psalm is filled with honest struggle, deep pain, tough questions, determined trust, and a biblical grounding. To learn how to lament, we must resolve to talk to God—to keep praying. I know that this sounds pretty basic, but it is where we have to start. Lament begins with an invitation to turn to God while in pain. Let me show you.

Cry Out to God

> I cry aloud to God,
>   aloud to God, and he will hear me.
> In the day of my trouble I seek the Lord;
>   in the night my hand is stretched out without
>   wearying;
>   my soul refuses to be comforted. (Ps. 77:1–2)

The opening line of this lament, "I cry aloud to God," frames the tone of the text. The psalmist is in pain, and yet he's not silent. However, he is not just talking, complaining, or whimpering; he's crying out in prayer.

Other references to prayer follow in the first two verses: "He will hear me" (v. 1b), "In the day of my trouble I seek the Lord" (v. 2a), and "In the night my hand is stretched out without wearying" (v. 2b) (a reference to a prayer posture).

Clearly the psalmist is reaching out to God in the midst of his pain. Please don't miss this or take it for granted. It's really important—in fact, it may be one of the reasons why you're reading this book.

It takes faith to pray a lament.

To pray in pain, even with its messy struggle and tough questions, is an act of faith where we open up our hearts to God. Prayerful lament is better than silence. However, I've found that many people are afraid of lament. They find it too honest, too open, or too risky. But there's something far worse:

silent despair. Giving God the silent treatment is the ultimate manifestation of unbelief. Despair lives under the hopeless resignation that God doesn't care, he doesn't hear, and nothing is ever going to change. People who believe this stop praying. They give up.

However, lament directs our emotions by prayerfully vocalizing our hurt, our questions, and even our doubt. Turning to prayer through lament is one of the deepest and most costly demonstrations of belief in God.[9] James Montgomery Boice (1938–2000), who pastored the Tenth Presbyterian Church in Philadelphia for thirty-two years, helps us see the spiritual value of praying through our spiritual questions:

> It is better to ask them than not to ask them, because asking them sharpens the issue and pushes us toward the right, positive response. Alexander Maclaren writes, "Doubts are better put into plain speech than lying diffused and darkening, like poisonous mists, in [the] heart. A thought, be it good or bad, can be dealt with when it is made articulate."[10]

I wonder how many believers stop speaking to God about their pain. Disappointed by unanswered prayers or frustrated by out-of-control circumstances, these people wind up in a spiritual desert unable—or refusing—to talk to God.

This silence is a soul killer.

Maybe you are one of those who've given God the silent treatment. Maybe you just don't know what to say. Perhaps there's a particular issue or struggle that you just can't talk to God about. It feels too painful. I hope you'll be encouraged to start praying again. Or perhaps you have a friend who is really

---

9. Card, *Sacred Sorrow*, 55.
10. James Montgomery Boice, *Psalms*, vol. 2, *Psalms 42–106*, An Expositional Commentary (Grand Rapids, MI: Baker, 2005), 640–41.

struggling in grief. Maybe this person prays some things that make you uncomfortable—even wince. But before you jump in too quickly and hush his or her prayer, remember that at least your friend is praying. It's a start.

Prayers of lament take faith.

Pray Your Struggles

However, praying in the midst of pain isn't a guarantee the emotional struggle will immediately lift. The psalmist's description of his ongoing tension is clear:

> My soul refuses to be comforted.
> When I remember God, I moan;
>   when I meditate, my spirit faints. Selah
>
> You hold my eyelids open;
>   I am so troubled that I cannot speak. (Ps. 77:2–4)

He's praying, but it's not bringing immediate comfort or resolution. His prayers are not "working." Yet, he still prays.

You need to know that lament does not always lead to an immediate solution. It does not always bring a quick or timely answer. Grief is not tame. Lament is not a simplistic formula. Instead, lament is the song you sing believing that *one day* God will answer and restore. Lament invites us to pray through our struggle with a life that is far from perfect.

Pray Your Questions

Painful circumstances surface big and troubling questions. The psalmist wrestles with why God isn't doing more. He begins to "consider the days of old," to "remember my song in the night," to "meditate in my heart," and to make "a diligent search" (77:5–6). He is thinking and reflecting.

This painful search leads to six pointed rhetorical questions:

1. "Will the Lord spurn forever?" (v. 7).
2. "Will [he] never again be favorable?" (v. 7).
3. "Has his steadfast love forever ceased?" (v. 8).
4. "Are his promises at an end for all time?" (v. 8).
5. "Has God forgotten to be gracious?" (v. 9).
6. "Has he in anger shut up his compassion?" (v. 9).

Does the psalmist really believe God isn't loving, doesn't keep his promises, and is unfaithful? I don't think so, and the rest of the psalm will bear this out. But he does something important here. Honestly praying this way recognizes that pain and suffering often create difficult emotions that are *not* based upon truth but *feel* true, nonetheless.

Honest, humble, pain-filled questions are part of what it means to be a follower of Jesus. We'll explore this more extensively in the next chapter when we learn about complaint. For now, I simply want you to see that lament is humbly turning to God through the pain. It takes faith to lay our painful questions before the Lord.

Anyone can cry, but it takes faith to turn to God in lament.

Prayer Turns Us Around

Lament is a prayer that leads us through personal sorrow and difficult questions into truth that anchors our soul. Psalm 77:11 includes an important and repeated word: "remember."

Then I said, "I will appeal to this,
to the years of the right hand of the Most High."

I will remember the deeds of the LORD;
yes, I will remember your wonders of old.

> I will ponder all your work,
>> and meditate on your mighty deeds. (Ps. 77:10–12)

This is where the lament prayer makes its turn toward resolution.

In all we feel and all the questions we have, there comes a point where we must call to mind what we know to be true. The entire psalm shifts with the word "then" in verse 10 and the subsequent appeal to the history of God's powerful deliverance.

Important phrases are connected to this remembrance: "I will appeal . . . / to the years of the right hand of the Most High" (v. 10), and "will remember the deeds of the LORD" (v. 11a). This reflection becomes personal, as if the psalmist is talking directly to God: "Yes, I will remember your wonders of old" (v. 11b), and

> I will ponder all your work,
>> and meditate on your mighty deeds. (v. 12)

He is looking back and reflecting on the works of God in the past.

Then the focus shifts again from the historical works of God to the very character of God.

> Your way, O God, is holy.
>> What god is great like our God? (v. 13)

Notice how different this rhetorical question is from the previous six questions! This is an important turning point. It makes lament full of grace as we turn from honest questions to confident trust.

The aim of this book is to help you understand this shift and to make it your own.

Earlier in this chapter I said that laments are possible only if you believe that God is truly good. You see, the character of God—his sovereignty, goodness, and love—creates a tension when we face painful circumstances.

Lament is how we learn to live between the poles of a hard life and God's goodness. It is an opportunity to remind our hearts about God's faithfulness in the past, especially when the immediate events of life are overwhelmingly negative. While we're still in pain, lament reminds our hearts of what we believe to be true.

Hurting people are given permission to grieve, but not aimlessly or selfishly. The biblical language of lament is able to redirect weeping people to what is true despite the valley they are walking through. I long for the experience of personal and corporate lament to be multiplied. How many Christians need to learn to lament? How many need to have their thinking redirected? I've come to love lament because of what it does in people's lives.

Pray the Gospel

Psalm 77 concludes with the ultimate moment that defined the people of Israel and their relationship with God: the exodus. The psalmist remembers this defining moment in Jewish history as God demonstrated his faithfulness and love:

> When the waters saw you, O God,
>> when the waters saw you, they were afraid;
>> indeed, the deep trembled. . . .
> Your way was through the sea,
>> your path through the great waters;
>> yet your footprints were unseen.
> You led your people like a flock
>> by the hand of Moses and Aaron. (vv. 16, 19–20)

Do you see what is happening here? The psalmist anchors his questioning, his hurting heart, to the single greatest redemptive event in the life of Israel. This moment defined his understanding of God's character. The exodus was an anchor for his weary soul.

For the Christian, the exodus event—the place where we find ultimate deliverance—is the cross of Christ. This is where all our questions—our heartaches and pain—should be taken. The cross shows us that God has already proven himself to be for us and not against us.

The apostle Paul even quotes a lament, Psalm 44, before proclaiming the promise that nothing can separate us from the love of God:

As it is written,

> "For your sake we are being killed all the day long;
>   we are regarded as sheep to be slaughtered."

No, in all these things we are more than conquerors through him who loved us. For I am sure that neither death nor life, nor angels nor rulers, nor things present nor things to come, nor powers, nor height nor depth, nor anything else in all creation, will be able to separate us from the love of God in Christ Jesus our Lord. (Rom. 8:36–39)

The promise for Christians is as glorious as it is deep:

Jesus bought the right to make everything right.

Even if we are "killed all day long" or are "like sheep going to the slaughter," nothing—no sorrow, no disappointment, no disease, no betrayal, not even death—can separate us from God's love.

Lament prayers celebrate this truth with tears.

Lament by Faith

Do you see now how uniquely Christian it is to lament? It takes faith to pray when you are in pain. Belief in God creates challenging questions, and lament provides the opportunity to reorient your hurting heart toward what is true. But in order for that to happen, you have to turn to prayer. The silent treatment must end. Frustration and discouragement might tempt you to stop talking to God.

Lament opens a door and shows you a path toward trust.

Heartfelt cries of lament are often brief or messy. They might feel a bit forced or uncomfortable. But keep talking to God. Don't allow your fear, your despair, or your track record of silence to cut off the flow of grace. Your pain can be a path toward God if you'll allow lament to be your new language.

If you don't have the words, read one of the psalms of lament out loud.[11] Linger over it. Let it open your heart. Let lament do its work in your life. Allow it to lead you to other aspects of this sacred song of sorrow. But whatever you do—don't stop talking to God. Keep wrestling. Keep struggling. Keep praying.

No one taught you how to cry. Tears are part of what it means to be human. But to lament is Christian. It is a prayer of faith for the journey between a hard life and God's goodness. We need to learn to lament. Through the tears, the first step is to turn to God in prayer.

Reflection Questions

1. In your own words, what makes lament Christian? Why does it take faith to lament?
2. Describe a time when you found it difficult to pray because you were suffering. What were the circumstances or the reasons for your silence?

---

11. See appendix 2 for a list of the various lament psalms.

3. What are some of the hard and painful questions that you've asked God over the years?

4. As you think back on God's faithfulness, where has he proven himself to be trustworthy?

5. What portions of Scripture do you use to anchor your soul to who God is?

6. How is lament connected to your theology?

7. How does the cross become the ultimate anchor and resolution for our suffering and pain?

8. Take a few minutes and talk to God about whatever is in your soul as you conclude this chapter. Tell him your pain, share your questions, affirm your trust, and ask him to keep you trusting.

2

Bring Your Complaints

Psalm 10

Why, O Lord, do you stand far away?
     Why do you hide yourself in times of trouble?

Psalm 10:1

"God, I know you're not mean, but it feels like you are today."

Sarah and I were sitting in our car outside our doctor's office. My wife's blunt prayer was all she could muster. We were devastated. Again.

This grief felt cruel.

Our previous appointment was to confirm a pregnancy after Sylvia's death. Two years and multiple miscarriages later, we were finally beyond the time frame of the prior failed pregnancies. We were filled with guarded hope. Our doctor ordered an ultrasound to confirm the new life in Sarah's womb.

We couldn't wait to see the flutter of a little heartbeat. This appointment was to be redemptive. I hoped it would bring closure.

But it only brought more pain.

The ultrasound room was too familiar—the same room where we learned of Sylvia's death. As the doctor began to move the wand over Sarah's womb, a shadow of concern crossed his face. Sarah watched carefully and noticed. She raised her head. "What is it?" she asked. I thought she was overreacting. I tried to reassure her. But the look on the doctor's face was now clear to me as well. Something was wrong.

"I don't know how to tell you this," our doctor said, "but there's no baby in your womb. Your hormone levels are good. There's a home, but there's no baby. It's called a blighted ovum—a false positive pregnancy." Sarah's head fell back. She sobbed. Again.

We walked—numb—to the car. I closed the door. We needed to pray. But what do you say in this moment? While I didn't understand it at the time, Sarah's prayer is what you'll find as you study lament. Her prayer was a complaint—an honest and blunt conversation with God. And in order for you to learn how to experience the mercy of lament, you need to learn to complain.

Godly Complaint

After we take the first step of turning to God in prayer, the next is bringing our complaints to him. There's a tension here. I'm sure you already feel it. *Complain* isn't a very positive word. We don't like complainers. It seems like the wrong response to situations where we should be content or thankful. But is that always the case? Is complaining always wrong?

It can't be.

If you read the psalms of lament, you'll discover a lot of creative complaining. You'll find expressions of sorrow, fear, frustration, and even confusion. In other words, the Bible is full of complaints. And apparently they aren't sinful. In fact, they were set to music as an entire congregation sang their frustration. Now, don't get me wrong. I'm not giving you permission to vent self-centered rage at God when life has not turned out like you planned. I'm not suggesting for a second you have a right to be angry with God. I think that is always wrong.

But I do think that there's a place for a kind of complaining that is biblical. In fact, bringing your complaints is central to lament. Todd Billings explains: "Writers of laments and complaints in the psalms often seek to make their 'case' against God, frequently citing God's promises in order to complain that God seems to be forgetting his promises. They throw the promises of God back at him."[1] You see, without a complaint, there would be no lament. Yet, I find the practice of godly complaint foreign to many Christians. This is one of the reasons why discovering lament is so needed.

Many people I know fall into one of two camps when walking through suffering: anger or denial. Some people are so filled with anger at God that they live in a self-made prison of despair and bitterness for the rest of their lives. Their pain gives rise to rage. And their spiritual life is never the same. Sometimes it even results in a complete rejection of Christianity as pain paves the way for unbelief.

Still others seem to think that godliness means a new form of stoicism. They try to project an air of contentment that feels like denial. "Everything's fine," they say. But you know it isn't. As I've dealt with many people in pain, I've often had to coax

---

1. Todd Billings, *Rejoicing in Lament: Wrestling with Incurable Cancer and Life in Christ* (Grand Rapids, MI: Brazos, 2015), 19.

them off the cliff of their anger or out of the cave of hiding their honest struggles.

Biblical lament offers an alternative. Through godly complaint we are able to express our disappointment and move toward a resolution. We complain on the basis of our belief in who God is and what he can do. As I said in chapter 1, the premise of this book is that, while crying is human, to lament is Christian. Lament is how those who know what God is like and believe in him address their pain. God is good, but life is hard. Enter complaint. Stacey Gleddiesmith provides a helpful explanation: "A lament honestly and specifically names a situation or circumstance that is painful, wrong, or unjust—in other words, a circumstance that does not align with God's character and therefore does not make sense within God's kingdom."[2]

Lament is the language of a people who believe in God's sovereignty but live in a world with tragedy. While writing this chapter, I've been involved in a funeral for a precious man who died suddenly of a heart attack, tracked the progress of a teenager who is fighting bone cancer, prayed for a woman who has to face her rapist in court, sought the Lord for a pregnant mom who learned she has breast cancer, and prayed for a young woman whose dad tried to take his life. Every one of these believers knows that God is good. They all believe he's in control. But life is still hard.

Part of the reason it's hard is that they believe the promises in the Scripture. They are fighting to trust in those promises through the tears. That was the tension Sarah was expressing in her tear-filled complaint. She believed in God's goodness—with all her heart. But a blighted ovum after a stillbirth and multiple miscarriages felt cruel. She was expressing godly complaint.

---

2. Stacey Gleddiesmith, "My God, My God, Why? Understanding the Lament Psalms," *Reformed Worship*, June 2010, www.reformedworship.org/article/june-2010/my-god-my-god-why.

Psalm 10: Start Complaining

If we are going to understand how to lament, and if we are going to discover the grace in it, we must learn how to complain the right way. To take this second step in learning to lament, let's look at Psalm 10 and a few other examples.

This psalm begins with two strong complaints:

> Why, O LORD, do you stand far away?
> Why do you hide yourself in times of trouble? (v. 1)

The problem of unresolved evil and injustice are the themes of this psalm. We don't know the specific background or the setting in which this was written. Some lament psalms were written because of a national crisis. Others were written because of personal problems. It appears that the psalmist is dealing with injustice, but he is also wrestling with God allowing it to remain unchallenged.

Bring Your Questions

"Why, O LORD, do you stand far away?" (Ps. 10:1) The psalmist is deeply troubled that God seems like he's too far removed from what is happening. The word for "LORD" here is the sacred and powerful name for God: Yahweh. It's the name that means "I AM," the name God gave Moses at the burning bush when he said, "Say this to the people of Israel: 'I AM has sent me to you'" (Ex. 3:14). This was the name of the God who delivered his people from the grip of the most powerful nation on earth. This was the God who made a mockery of the false gods of Egypt, turning them against their worshipers in the ten plagues. This was the same God who led Israel through the wilderness and who inhabited the tabernacle. This was the God who defended his people and delivered them. Yahweh was a deliverer. He parted the Red Sea. He brought his people out of slavery (Ex. 20:1–2).

However, in this moment, God seems to the psalmist to be standing "far away." Feel the language. God's people are in trouble, and it feels as if God is distant. The psalmist fears that God is no longer helping him.

When was the last time you felt like this? I'm sure you know not only the pain of suffering but also the struggle with God's seeming remoteness. I think every believer can relate to this at some point in his or her life. The lament psalms teach us that these feelings should not be dismissed as invalid or sinful. They are part of the journey—an aspect of genuine faith.

The second question is even more pointed. "Why do you hide yourself in times of trouble?" (Ps. 10:1). This complaint moves to an accusation of active disinterest. It's not just that God is standing far away. Now the problem is the feeling that God is hiding himself. The word "hiding" can mean secret, hidden, and concealed. But it also can have more emotional meanings, such as withdrawn, ignoring, and pretending to be one thing while actually being another.[3]

Does this make you at all uncomfortable? It should. The psalmist is basically telling God that he feels as if God is not being God-like. If you are comfortable with this, then you probably don't understand what is said here. The psalmist is deeply struggling, and not just with his pain; he's struggling with God. Injustice is one thing, but God's lack of intervention is a deeper pain—one that creates complaint.

This second step in lament is helpful because it speaks to something familiar. All of us eventually discover that life is filled with unfairness. Have you ever been wronged by someone? Have you ever watched as people were unfairly treated? That

---

3. James Swanson, *Dictionary of Biblical Languages with Semantic Domains: Hebrew (Old Testament)* (Oak Harbor, IL: Logos Research Systems, 1997), word 6623.

is painful enough. What makes the situation even more challenging is when the perpetrator seems to get away with it. The lack of consequences or resolution is maddening.

Complaint gives voice to our hard questions.

Life is filled with a variety of suffering. Pain comes in many forms. Lament speaks into all the sorrows of life—no matter how small or big. Sorrow could enter your life because of unfulfilled longings, loneliness, an ailing body, or an unfair supervisor at work. It could come in the form of a job loss, financial struggles, a broken engagement, or ongoing conflict in a marriage. Our hearts can groan under the weight of infertility, cancer, a failed adoption, an adulterous spouse, or wayward children. The longer we live, the more pain we see. God could intervene, but there are times—many times—when he chooses not to. That's the tension of complaint.

Psalm 10, however, is not the only place vocalizing this struggle. As you read other psalms, you'll see God often addressed in complaint language. Frequently it is connected to questions, including plenty of *why* questions. A few examples:

> My God, my God, why have you forsaken me?
>   Why are you so far from saving me . . . ? (Ps. 22:1)

> Awake! Why are you sleeping, O Lord? . . .
>   Why do you forget our affliction and oppression?
>   (Ps. 44:23–24)

> Why then have you broken down its [Jerusalem's]
>   walls . . . ? (Ps. 80:12)

> O Lord, why do you cast my soul away? (Ps. 88:14)

Looking further, you find a number of other complaints connected to *how* question:

How long, O LORD? Will you forget me forever?
　　How long will you hide your face from me? . . .
How long shall my enemy be exalted over me?
　　　(Ps. 13:1–2)

How long, O Lord, will you look on? (Ps. 35:17)

How long, O God, is the foe to scoff?
　　Is the enemy to revile your name forever? (Ps. 74:10)

O LORD, how long shall the wicked,
　　how long shall the wicked exult? (Ps. 94:3)

How shall we sing the LORD's song
　　in a foreign land? (Ps. 137:4)

Once you start to see these questions in the Psalms, they jump off the page. These heartfelt questions have been in your Bible all along, but somehow they've been easy to miss. It is almost as if we don't understand the value of bringing our questions to God. Perhaps we think they're not allowed. Michael Jinkins, in his book *In the House of the Lord*, reminds us that God can handle our struggles:

> The psalms of lament open us to the greatness of a God who not only can hear, but also can handle our pain, our self-pity, our blame, and our fear, who can respond to our anger, our disillusionment in the midst of oppression and persecution, under the boot of tyranny and our sense of God-forsakenness in the face of life's most profound alienations and exiles.[4]

These psalms give us permission—even encouragement—to lay out our struggles, even if they are with God himself.

---

4. Michael Jinkins, *In the House of the Lord: Inhabiting the Psalms of Lament* (Collegeville, MN: Liturgical, 1989), 39.

A few years ago I taught on a few psalms of lament at our church. Afterward a man asked for an appointment to talk with me. During our meeting, he told me about his lifelong struggle with same-sex attraction. He was discouraged with the counseling he had received. From his perspective, well-meaning counselors had worked with him to change only his behavior. It was always a "temporary fix." Before long he would fall back into the same pattern of sinful behavior.

When I asked him why we were meeting, he told me that the words from the lament psalms seemed to be pulled from his journal. He felt like God had forgotten him. He struggled with why God allowed some very painful circumstances in his childhood to occur. He battled anger with his parents. He felt like God was always distant. His struggle was not only with same-sex attraction but also with God.

I remember the look in his eyes when I told him, "Well, it sounds like the psalm from Sunday was written for you. But it also sounds like you've not journeyed through the text yet." Over the next few months, along with Scripture memorization and Bible Study—all the things he'd tried before— I encouraged him to tell God exactly how he was feeling. I challenged him to complain—to lay out his pain, his questions, and his struggles before the Lord. I tried to help him see that not only could God handle his messy thoughts; he already knew them. The struggling man's questions were not a surprise to God.

Slowly the darkness began to lift in this brother's life. The struggle with same-sex attraction didn't vanish, but his sense of divine abandonment did. As he poured out his soul in lament, it opened his heart for God to apply healing grace in his life. The painful questions that once created a barrier between him and God now became the vehicle to draw him closer to the One who would change his heart. Questions in lament became the means by which God began a work of renewal in his life. He started to change.

Complaint was part of that journey.

Bring Your Frustrations

Asking God questions is not the only aspect of biblical complaint. Psalm 10 also shows us the value of telling God our frustrations. There is something helpful and right about regularly laying out the specifics of our pain. In Psalm 10, we see this clearly. We see the cause of his complaint:

- "In arrogance the wicked hotly pursue the poor" (v. 2).
- "The wicked boasts of the desires of his soul" (v. 3).
- "The one greedy for gain curses and renounces the LORD" (v. 3).
- "In the pride of his face the wicked does not seek him" (v. 4).
- "All his thoughts are, 'There is no God'" (v. 4).

The psalmist is outraged with the wicked actions of the proud. He is frustrated that there seems to be no justice. It appears that the proud and oppressive person only knows success!

> His ways prosper at all times;
>> your judgments are on high, out of his sight. (v. 5)

The oppressor acts as if he'll never experience adversity (v. 6). His mouth is full of cursing (v. 7). He lies in wait and plans for his next victim (vv. 8–9). Vulnerable people are hurt by his actions (v. 10). The proud man concludes,

> God has forgotten,
>> he has hidden his face, he will never see it. (v. 11)

However, the psalmist turns his powerless position into a platform to call out to God. His blunt complaint is an opportunity to redirect his heart. Rather than allowing painful circumstances to rule him, creating bitterness or despair, he lays out his angst. The specificity sharpens the prayer. The frustrations expressed in lament push him further toward God, not away.

Discovering this practice of laying out my frustrations in candid terms has been life-giving. There were some days after the loss of Sylvia when I would wake up feeling frustrated. My first emotions of those days were dark. Few things are more unhelpful than being assaulted with discouragement as you climb out of bed. But through this, I learned the value of simply telling the Lord what was running through my soul. The more clear and blunt I could be, the better. Sometimes I wrestled to put words to what I was feeling because, frankly, I was embarrassed. I had to remind myself often that my struggles were not a surprise to God.

Some days I would list in a journal everything that was troubling me. My practice was to write out a list of complaints and then to talk to God about them. I found that pain made me myopic. It tended to narrow my focus on the sorrow that took over my life. Nothing else mattered. At least it felt that way. With this desperation for relief, it was easy to become preoccupied with the weight of sorrow, the unfairness of life, or the fear of never being happy again. Left unchecked, this could create a self-focused emotional spiral. But as I wrote out my complaints and talked to the Lord about them, it was surprising how they lost their hold on me. Sometimes I even found myself laughing at the silly things I listed. Complaint helped me see myself and my situation more clearly. Since then I've made it a regular practice to talk to God more quickly about my questions and frustrations.

The pain of stillbirth and the blighted ovum created a new and redemptive language for me. Over time I began to love lament—even complaint—because of where it led me. I learned that candid complaint has the potential to lead into the next steps of lament: asking and trusting. We'll look at these in the two chapters that follow. For now, I simply want you to see how complaint is more than a series of grievances. It is a path for reorienting your thinking and your feelings.

How to Complain the Right Way

I've spent the bulk of this chapter trying to make the case for biblical complaint. My hope is that you are more convinced than when you started reading, and that the next time you walk through any pain, you'll use biblical complaining to reorient your heart.

In order to help you get started, here are a few steps in learning how to complain the right way:

Come Humble

If you're going to offer a complaint to God, it must be done with a humble heart. As I said before, I don't think there is ever a place to be angry with God. However, I do think it's permissible to ask pain-filled questions as long as you're coming in humility. Proud, demanding questions from a heart that believes it is owed something from God will never lean into true lament. Before you start complaining, be sure you've checked arrogance at the door. Come with your pain, not your pride.

Pray the Bible

As I discovered this minor-key song, I memorized a favorite lament from the Psalms. I did so because the verses captured the essence of my struggle, and I needed the boundary of biblical language to keep my lament on track. I found poignant language that I could pray back to God. Maybe you need to do the same thing. To help you, I've made a list of twenty complaints in appendix 1. Perhaps that's a place for you to start. Or maybe that list will help you find one particular lament psalm that could give you words which capture the struggle in your soul. Remember, the lament psalms are there for a reason. Start complaining by praying the Bible.

Be Honest

I've mentioned this already, but it bears repeating. Biblical complaint doesn't work if you aren't honest with God about your pain, your fears, or your frustrations. Talk to him as a loving Father. Remember that you have a Savior who understands your struggles (Heb. 4:15). Remember, Jesus prayed, "My God, my God why have you forsaken me?" (Matt. 27:46). Take comfort from that. What's more, we have the Spirit of God who intercedes for us with "groanings too deep for words" (Rom. 8:26). The triune God is not surprised by your struggles or your frustrations. So tell him. Tell all of it— humbly and honestly.

Don't Just Complain

Finally, let me give you a word of caution. While you shouldn't skip the practice of complaint, you also shouldn't get stuck there either. Complaint was never meant to be an end in itself. In other words, lament does not give you an excuse to wallow in your questions or frustrations. It is a means to another end. In the same way a surgeon's cut is meant to heal, so complaint is designed to move us along in our lament. You are not meant to linger in complaint. If you never move beyond complaint, lament loses its purpose and its power.

Complaint is central to lament. But Christians never complain just to complain. Instead, we bring our complaints to the Lord for the purpose of moving us toward him. We allow the honest opening of our souls to become a doorway to the other elements of lament.

I don't know why you've picked up this book, but I would guess that you have some pain in your life that could become prayers of complaint. Before you move on to the next two chapters, maybe you need to take a few minutes and talk to the Lord about the challenges in your soul. Maybe you need to start with this prayer: "God, I know you are not _____, but it feels like you are today."

Complaint is a turning point of lament. Be honest. Talk to God about your struggles. Even if it's messy or embarrassing, let biblical complaining push you toward what comes next: asking God for help.

Reflection Questions

1. Before reading this chapter, what was your perspective on complaining to God?
2. Why is complaint a central element of lament?
3. What was surprising about the *why* and *how* questions in the Psalms? What was comforting and encouraging about the list?
4. What are some reasons Christians are reluctant to voice their complaints to God in prayer?
5. How is complaining the right way spiritually helpful?
6. Make a list of the kinds of complaints you've offered or should have offered to the Lord.
7. Take some time to thank the Lord for allowing us to be honest with him.
8. When is complaint sinful and wrong?
9. Is there a complaint that you need to humbly offer to the Lord today?

3

Ask Boldly

Psalm 22

> Be not far from me,
>   for trouble is near,
>   and there is none to help.

Psalm 22:11

Thankfully, the prayer of complaint in the parking lot was not the end of our story. A few months later Sarah was pregnant again. Back in the dreaded ultrasound room, we could see the grainy flutter of a heartbeat and the clear formation of a little body. Life!

I wanted desperately to be relieved. I hoped to be happy. But I wasn't. I was frightened. After so much pain and disappointment, my heart was jaded. I was not only afraid of losing another child. I was scared to hope again.

The months that followed brought a new set of challenges. Sarah and I battled fear nearly every day. Discouragement and anxiety seemed to lurk around every corner. Each doctor's appointment brought terrible memories back as we waited to hear our unborn baby's heartbeat. We made multiple emergency room trips, fearing that our baby hadn't moved, only to learn that everything was fine.

Our new normal was a brutal fight.

Throughout this long journey, I was meeting weekly with a group of pastors to pray for revival in our city. This multidenominational, city-wide prayer initiative connected me to dozens of pastors from various evangelical churches. I developed deep friendships as we sought the Lord together.

One blessing of this brotherhood was an annual prayer retreat. For three days we gathered at a conference center to seek the Lord through worship-based prayer. One particular moment was life changing. It shaped my understanding of lament.

During one of our group prayer times, I began to lament my fears about Sarah's pregnancy. Our fight for faith left me exhausted. My soul was weary. In front of the other pastors I talked candidly to the Lord about my daily battle. I laid out my anxiety, struggles, and doubts. It was a brutally honest lament. After I finished my tear-filled complaint, a few pastors gathered around me. They began to pray.

A pastor named Bernie placed his thick hand on my chest. He prayed with bold confidence: "God, I call on you to give strength to my brother!" As he leaned into me, it felt as if he was pushing his prayer into my heart. He prayed again. This time louder. "I pray for strength for my brother." Then almost shouting: "Strength for my brother!"

As I was circled by these pastors in prayer, something happened in my soul. Bernie's prayer was filled with such confidence in the Lord. He called on God with an authority that was strangely refreshing. My fear didn't vanish, but Bernie's confidence in God became mine.

My heartfelt complaint was eclipsed by his bold request.

Psalm 22: Asking Boldly

So far we've learned that lament involves turning to prayer and giving voice to our complaints. I've tried to help you see the need to keep praying through your pain, whatever the reason. In the previous chapter, we learned about the spiritual value of bringing our complaints to God. Now we come to the third step: asking boldly.

This next leg in our journey involves confidently calling upon God to act in accordance with his character. It is how lament moves from the *why* question of complaint to the *who* question of request. As I read through the lament psalms, I think of my friend Bernie. The writers are equally bold in their requests. They call upon God with such authority that it seems as if they're commanding God to act. Their confidence in God's character and their knowledge of his past deliverance compel them to make bold requests. The writers of lament stake their claim on what God has promised to do.

However, these requests do something more. Boldly asking God for help based upon who he is and what he's promised eclipses the complaints. I say "eclipses" for a reason. It captures the fact that *why* questions are not always answered before we move into requests. Just as one heavenly body moves into the shadow of another during an eclipse, so too the *why* questions and the *who* questions coexist, but not equally.[1] Who God is becomes the more prominent reality while not

---

1. For this image of an eclipse, I'm thankful to Debbie Ambruster, email correspondence, November 4, 2017.

removing the lingering questions. As we make our bold requests, "Why is this happening?" moves into the shadow of "Who is God?"

That's why we need to ask boldly.

I'm not sure you can find a more well-known *why* question in the Bible than Psalm 22:1. In the final moments of Jesus's agony on the cross, he quoted David's lament (Matt. 27:46; Mark 15:34). Psalm 22 is unique because it combines the first two steps of lament (turn and complain) in the first two verses. It is powerful because it immediately launches into agony:

> My God, my God, why have you forsaken me?
>> Why are you so far from saving me, from the words of
>>> my groaning?
> O my God, I cry by day, but you do not answer,
>> and by night, but I find no rest. (vv. 1–2)

The Yet Bridge

This lament is striking because immediately following these two very pointed complaints, David turns to God's character. The key word is *yet*. It becomes a bridge that leads from complaint to bold requests. Don't miss it!

> Yet you are holy,
>> enthroned on the praises of Israel.
> In you our fathers trusted;
>> they trusted, and you delivered them.
> To you they cried and were rescued;
>> in you they trusted and were not put to shame.
>>> (Ps. 22:3–5)

After David rehearses the cruel mocking that is causing him pain in verses 6–8, we again find the word *yet*:

Yet you are he who took me from the womb;
>   you made me trust you at my mother's breasts.
On you was I cast from my birth,
>   and from my mother's womb you have been my God.
>   (vv. 9–10)

Do you see what David is doing? In his deep pain and his sense of abandonment, he anchors his soul to who God is and what he has done. Later we'll see David make his bold requests despite the waves of questions and the rising tide of frustrations. His complaints are not cul-de-sacs of sorrow but bridges that lead him to God's character. This is why we love the Psalms, especially lament psalms! They anchor us to the *yet* of God's character.

In my study of lament, I've come to love the word *yet*. It marks the place in the journey where pain and belief coexist. It is how we gain the confidence to ask boldly, despite the sorrow and grief we feel. *Yet* means that I choose to keep asking God for help, to cry out to him for my needs, even when the pain of life is raw. *Yet* reminds us that sorrow doesn't have to yield before we ask God for help. Part of the grace of lament is the way it invites us to pray boldly even when we are bruised badly.

Is there anything you have stopped asking God to do in your life? Has the pain of circumstances or have the disappointments of unanswered prayers led you to a resigned silence as to what you want to see God do? Maybe *yet* can become your new favorite word in the Bible. Perhaps it could be the bridge that leads you to make your request with a new level of confidence.

Bold Requests

With the character of God in the forefront of his thoughts, David now makes his bold requests in Psalm 22:11–21. He needs God's help. This lament is filled with urgency and expectation. Look at what David says:

Be not far from me,
>   for trouble is near,
>   and there is none to help. . . .

But you, O LORD, do not be far off!
>   O you my help, come quickly to my aid!
Deliver my soul from the sword,
>   my precious life from the power of the dog!
>   Save me from the mouth of the lion!
You have rescued me from the horns of the wild oxen!
>   (vv. 11, 19–21)

Notice how each request confidently calls upon God to act. It is striking. The character of God, combined with the desperation of pain, pushes David to be bold.

We pray differently when we're hurting and desperate. I'm sure you know what I'm talking about. Pain has a way of awakening us to our need for God's help. It shines a spotlight on our powerlessness to control everything. We are never more aware of our frailty than when hardship comes our way. This is one of the blessings of suffering if we allow lament to lead us. The various trials of life can become a platform to reaffirm our dependence upon the Lord. The requests of lament can become the place where we celebrate our need for God's help. In this way, our requests become more than just expressions of need. These petitions are prayers of faith anchored in what we believe about God.

Have you ever prayed with individuals as bold as my friend Bernie? As you listened to their prayers and heard their confident cries to God, is it not true that you were drawn into their confidence? Their boldness fanned the flame of belief within your prayer life. Bold requests create more boldness.

The point of those requests is not only to meet a need. The point is to rely upon God.

But What Do We Ask For?

Beyond Psalm 22, there are many types of requests in the lament psalms. The uniqueness of painful circumstances is reflected in the variety of bold requests. These pain-filled petitions in lament are as diverse as the stories of the people who will read this book. That is one of the reasons why we run to the Psalms, especially lament psalms. They live where we live.

However, the diversity is also helpful at a personal level. The requests of lament are as unique as the circumstances that invade the span of our lives. As new seasons of sorrow arrive, the lament psalms help us know what and how to pray through every season.

A survey of the unique petitions in these songs of sorrow shows us at least nine different prayers. Together these serve as a model for what we can pray. As you consider the variety of these requests, they can create a new level of confidence—even motivation—to reach out to God and to keep asking, regardless of the situation you're facing. Let these bold requests become your own.

1. *"Arise, O LORD!"* Seven lament psalms call upon God to "arise" or "rise up" (Psalms 3, 7, 9, 10, 17, 74, 94). These laments plead with God to fix what is wrong with the world. For example:

Arise, O LORD; O God, lift up your hand;
    forget not the afflicted. (Ps. 10:12)

We know that if God is moved to act, everything will change. Therefore, we should ask for divine intervention. In effect we should say: "Do something, Lord! Please!"

2. *"Grant us help."* Suffering of any kind confronts our self-sufficiency. We are always dependent upon God's help, but pain makes that gap real. The lament psalms are filled with cries for deliverance, rescue, and strength. For instance:

Oh, grant us help against the foe,
    for vain is the salvation of man!
With God we shall do valiantly;
    it is he who will tread down our foes. (Ps. 60:11–12)

By asking God for help, we are not only marshaling the resources of an omnipotent God; we are also reminding our hearts that God can be trusted.

3. *"Remember your covenant."* When the Bible calls upon God to remember, it's not that he has forgotten. Instead, it's a way of asking God to be true to the promises he's made. This request tells God, "I'm trusting in what your Word says, Lord!" It fights against the temptation to believe only what we can see with our eyes. Asking God to remember connects our present struggle to God's historic faithfulness.

Remember your mercy, O LORD, and your steadfast love,
    for they have been from of old. (Ps. 25:6)

4. *"Let justice be done."*

Fill their faces with shame
    that they may seek your name . . .
    let them perish in disgrace
that they may know that you alone . . .
    are the Most High. (Ps. 83:16–18)

Some laments are what theologians call imprecatory psalms. They long for the punishment of the wicked. When you face injustice, and when God's glory—not just your pain—is your focus, it is appropriate to ask for justice to be done. Blunt requests for the defeat of the wicked have often been the prayers of godly people. Lament gives us language for talking to God about unfairness, abuse, and hidden mistreatment. We can boldly call upon God to act for the sake of justice.

5. *"Don't remember our sins."* Sometimes the situation behind our lament is directly connected to our sins. For example, David's high-handed sins of adultery and murder prompted Psalm 51 to be written. At other times, the transgressions of an entire nation are to blame. We'll see this corporate grief when we look at the book of Lamentations in part 2.

The request that God not remember our sins simply asks that God would not treat us as our sins deserve. It appeals for God's mercy and grace:

> Have mercy on me, O God,
> > according to your steadfast love;
> according to your abundant mercy
> > blot out my transgressions. (Ps. 51:1)

> Do not remember against us our former iniquities;
> > let your compassion come speedily to meet us,
> > for we are brought very low.
> Help us, O God of our salvation,
> > for the glory of your name;
> deliver us, and atone for our sins,
> > for your name's sake! (Ps. 79:8–9)

When our sin is the cause of our lament, it's good to know that we can still ask for God's mercy.

6. *"Restore us!"* A number of lament psalms feature a request for God to bring restoration. For example:

> Restore us, O God;
> > let your face shine, that we may be saved! (Ps. 80:3)

The big-picture narrative of the gospel anticipates ultimate restoration in the new heavens and the new earth. This theme is woven through Scripture from Genesis to Revelation. Lament yearns for the fulfillment of this future reality. It could be your longing for restoration in your soul, your marriage, your family, your church, or your nation—or the final restoration of the world with the permanent removal of pain and brokenness. Regardless, this request asks God to bring spiritual healing at any level and in any area.

7. *"Don't be silent—listen to me."* As you become more familiar with requests in the psalms of lament, you'll notice how often God's silence is mentioned. For example, Psalm 28 combines these concerns into a personal request:

> To you, O Lord, I call;
>> my rock, be not deaf to me,
> lest, if you be silent to me,
>> I become like those who go down to the pit.
> Hear the voice of my pleas for mercy. (Ps. 28:1–2)

If you've felt the deafening silence of heaven, reach out to the Lord and ask him for help. If you battle the dismay of wondering whether God still hears, keep pouring out your requests. Don't stop asking. Say to the Lord,

> Give ear, O Lord, to my prayer;
>> listen to my plea for grace. (Ps. 86:6)

8. *"Teach me."* Pain has a way of getting our attention. It can be a wake-up call, a unique opportunity for spiritual growth. We'll unpack this more fully when we look at Lamentations. However, a number of lament psalms ask the Lord to teach us:

> Teach me to do your will,
>> for you are my God! (Ps. 143:10)

So teach us to number our days
    that we may get a heart of wisdom. (Ps. 90:12)

Teach me your way, O Lord,
    that I may walk in your truth;
    unite my heart to fear your name. (Ps. 86:11)

What about you? What do you need to ask the Lord to teach you through your struggle? Requests like these help us not waste our trials.

9. *"Vindicate me."* One of the most personal requests relates to the desire to defend yourself. If you've ever been falsely accused, misunderstood, or unfairly treated, you know the desperate desire to set the record straight. Rather than going down the path of bitterness or counterpunching, lament psalms give us a place to ask God for the vindication we desire—and even rightly deserve.

Awake and rouse yourself for my vindication,
    for my cause, my God and my Lord!
Vindicate me, O Lord, my God,
    according to your righteousness,
    and let them not rejoice over me! (Ps. 35:23–24)

This kind of request can become a balm for your soul as you keep entrusting yourself to One who judges justly (1 Pet. 2:23).

———

Did you know that this variety of bold requests existed in lament psalms? These petitions are as unique as the circumstances that create pain. I hope you're encouraged by this. Lament is an expansive prayer language. It can be your companion through a wide spectrum of struggles and challenges. God invites us, in every season and through every pain, to lay out our needs—to call upon him with confidence.

Ask the Man of Sorrows

In the New Testament, Christians are invited—even commanded—to ask boldly. The writer of Hebrews says, "Let us then with confidence draw near to the throne of grace, that we may receive mercy and find grace to help in time of need" (Heb. 4:16). What is the basis of this confidence? Why should we bring our heartfelt requests to God? The answer is connected to Jesus's experience of the brokenness of our world and his sympathy. We ask boldly because he understands deeply. "For we do not have a high priest who is unable to sympathize with our weaknesses" (Heb. 4:15).

Jesus was a man of sorrows and acquainted with grief. The New Testament often connects his statements or actions to lament psalms. For example, when describing Jesus's disgust with the injustice and perversion of temple worship in John 2:17, John cites the lament of Psalm 69:9 for context: "Zeal for your house has consumed me." When Jesus talked about betrayal in John 13:18, again a lament psalm is quoted: "He who ate my bread has lifted his heel against me" (see Ps. 41:9). And as I've mentioned before, Jesus quoted Psalm 22:1, "Why have you forsaken me?" on the cross. In other words, Jesus lived a life of lament. He knows the sorrows of injustice, hypocrisy, false accusations, physical weakness, temptations, betrayal, and feeling abandoned. That becomes the basis for our bold requests.

Songs of sorrow and the Man of Sorrows meet us in our pain. They invite us to keep asking with bold confidence. No matter what the situation or the pain, they call us to move from *why* to *who* by calling upon God to act.

Boldness Begets Boldness

The lament psalms have become like my friend Bernie to me over the years. To be honest, there are many days when my requests feel really weak. The angst in my soul seems to be stronger than my confidence in God. That's when I need the bold confidence of biblical lamenters. That's when I allow the requests of the psalms of lament to buoy my faith.

Their boldness begets boldness in me.

Beyond your own prayers, keep this in mind the next time you are walking alongside a hurting friend. You might think that praying with someone in pain is a small and insignificant thing, but it's not. You'll likely be able to ask God for help with a different level of faith than your hurting friend can muster. The boldness of your request and the confidence in your approach to the throne of grace can be a great help. You can pray with a firm belief that creates stronger faith in others. If you don't know what to pray, consider appealing to God through the words of a lament like Psalm 13 or 22. As you echo the boldness of the psalm, it can beget boldness in a hurting friend.

I've seen this happen in our church as we've put lament into practice. During one of our monthly prayer gatherings the focus was prodigal children. We invited hurting parents to cry out to the Lord for their wayward kids. The service was full. I was blown away by the response. This was a uniquely painful issue.

During our prayer time, I invited parents of prodigals to kneel at the front of the sanctuary. They came in droves. The tears started immediately. As they gathered around the platform, I invited them to call out—one at a time—the name of their wayward son or daughter. It was remarkable how much sorrow you can hear in just a name uttered by a broken parent. The level of grief was overwhelming.

What happened next was beautiful. I invited friends of those who were kneeling to gather around them and to pray boldly for the return of these children. I knew most of the parents would be weary with unanswered prayers. Many would struggle to believe God would answer. With hands laid on the shoulders of weeping parents, brothers and sisters in Christ lifted up their confident, bold prayers. They asked the Lord to hear them, to change the hearts of sons and daughters, and to bring them home. As a chorus of these groans filled the room, I could see the nodding of parents' heads all around the sanctuary platform. The weariness of grieving parents was eclipsed by the boldness of those who had entered their lament. As with Bernie's prayer for me, the pain didn't vanish, but the confidence of others became their own.

Lament invites us to ask boldly. We are given permission to lay out our pain and to call on God to intervene. This third step in lament moves us from *why* to *who*. The wide variety of requests in the lament psalms help us to see that no matter what the pain or how long the struggle, we need to keep asking.

What daunting need is staring you down? Whatever it is, talk to God about it. Confidently ask him to help you. Don't allow the pain or struggle to halt the lament journey by wallowing in your complaints. Call God to act! Ask him for the grace, the mercy, and the provision you need.

Let the boldness of the lament psalms fuel your confidence in God. Allow these songs of sorrow to push spiritual strength into your soul.

Keep asking—boldly. And then move to the final step in lament: choosing to trust.

Reflection Questions

1. What would happen if a person stopped the lament process with complaint and didn't move toward asking boldly?

2. Do you have a personal experience similar to mine with Bernie? How did the confidence of another believer's prayer help your faith?

3. How can bold requests move us from focusing on *why* to focusing on *who*? Why is that important?

4. Why is the word *yet* so important in Psalm 22? Write out your own sentence expressing pain but also including a personal statement that moves through *yet* to who God is.

5. Review the four requests in Psalm 22 and the nine categories. Which prayers are most meaningful to you, and why?

6. In light of the present struggle you are facing, what bold request(s) do you need to pray?

7. How might a community of believers be helpful in praying boldly?

8. How could this chapter change the way you help a person who is grieving and struggling?

4

Choose to Trust

Psalm 13

But I have trusted in your steadfast love;
    my heart shall rejoice in your salvation.
I will sing to the Lord,
    because he has dealt bountifully with me.

Psalm 13:5–6

"All true songs of worship are born in the wilderness of suffering," says musician and author Michael Card.[1] In reflecting on the laments of David, Card suggests that without the "rocky terrain of his lonely life," we would not have many of the psalms of David that we cherish.[2] In other words, David's pain created his worshipful laments. I think Card is right. Suffering refines what we trust in and how we talk about it.

---

1. Michael Card, *A Sacred Sorrow: Reaching Out to God in the Lost Language of Lament* (Colorado Springs: NavPress, 2005), 63.

2. Card, *Sacred Sorrow*, 63.

Pain can bring clarity.

Loss affirms trust.

Maybe that's why the words of the English poet William Cowper (1731–1800) are so full of meaning and depth. Cowper (pronounced Cooper) struggled with debilitating bouts of depression, even landing him in an insane asylum for a time.[3] Most of his life he wrestled with how to turn his sorrow into trust. Aside from composing beloved hymns such as "There Is a Fountain Filled with Blood" and "O for a Closer Walk with God," Cowper wrote "God Moves in a Mysterious Way" in 1774. It is believed to be the last hymn he wrote.[4]

God moves in a mysterious way
    His wonders to perform;
He plants his footsteps in the sea,
    And rides upon the storm.

Deep in unfathomable mines
    Of never-failing skill,
He treasures up his bright designs,
    And works his sovereign will.

Ye fearful saints, fresh courage take,
    The clouds ye so much dread
Are big with mercy, and shall break
    In blessings on your head!

Judge not the Lord by feeble sense,
    But trust him for his grace:
Behind a frowning providence
    He hides a smiling face.

3. John Piper, *The Hidden Smile of God: The Fruit of Affliction in the Lives of John Bunyan, William Cowper, and David Brainerd* (Wheaton, IL: Crossway, 2001), 92.

4. Hymnary.org, accessed July 25, 2018, https://hymnary.org/text/god_moves_in_a _mysterious_way.

His purposes will ripen fast,
   Unfolding every hour;
The bud may have a bitter taste,
   But sweet will be the flower.

Blind unbelief is sure to err,
   And scan his work in vain:
God is his own interpreter,
   And he will make it plain![5]

This hymn has been a refuge to me. I appreciate its candid statements about dreaded clouds, judging the Lord with feeble sense, and the category of "frowning providence." Cowper clearly lived in the real world of human sorrow.

But I love this hymn because of Cowper's ability to turn from hardship to the character of God: fearful clouds are full of mercy; a frowning providence hides a smiling face.

Pain can become a platform for worship.

Suffering can lead to trust. Lament is the language for this transition. Songs of sorrow are meant to move us from complaint to confidence in God.

It's Time to Choose

From the beginning of our journey, my goal has been to help you envision where lament leads. We've reached our destination. I hope you sense the opportunity that's before you. But you're going to have make the choice to take this final step. Unfortunately, I know far too many people who are stuck in their complaints. Others never move beyond their requests and what they want God to do for them. I hope you'll be different. While I've tried to encourage you to talk to God about your

5. H. Stebbing, *The Complete Poetical Works of William Cowper* (New York: D. Appleton, 1869), 404–5.

struggles and to ask boldly for what you need, now you will need to bring lament to its appropriate conclusion.

You will need to choose to trust.

While I can't make that decision for you, I know lament can help lead you there. This prayer language is divinely designed to guide you to the spiritual safe harbor of confidence in God and praising his name. Reaching out to God in prayer, laying your complaints before him, and boldly asking for help were meant to bring you to this point: to invite you to make the decision of faith-filled worship.

Trust = Active Patience

Now don't make the mistake of thinking that trust is something you decide once and for all as you are walking through pain. It's not as if you pray one lament prayer, and you never need to lament again. Life isn't that simple. Grief is not that tame. Instead, we must enter into lament over and over so that it can keep leading us to trust.

In this respect, lament allows us to embrace an endurance that is not passive. Lament helps us to practice active patience.[6] Trust looks like talking to God, sharing our complaints, seeking God's help, and then recommitting ourselves to believe in who God is and what he has done—even as the trial continues. Lament is how we endure. It is how we trust. It is how we wait. Rebekah Eklund provides this helpful summary: "The prayer of lament rejoices in God's saving actions in the now and hopes urgently for God's saving actions in the future, the 'not yet' of the eschatological timeline. . . . Those who lament stand on the boundary between the old age and the new and hope for things unseen."[7]

---

6. I'm grateful for Rebekah Eklund's category of nonpassive patience, which I changed to active patience here. See Rebekah Ann Eklund, "Lord, Teach Us How to Grieve: Jesus' Laments and Christian Hope," (ThD diss., Duke Divinity School, 2012).

7. Eklund, "Lord, Teach Us How to Grieve," 276.

This is one reason why I'm passionate about lament. It has the possibility of providing a pathway and a language that allow people not only to deal with the reality of their pain but also to be refocused on the trustworthiness of God. As we wait for future deliverance, our spiritual posture need not be passive. While there may be painful circumstances beyond our control, our waiting can be spiritually productive as we intentionally follow the pathway to trust. That is why trust is active patience.

We keep trusting by lamenting.

Psalm 13: Choosing to Trust

In this chapter we'll look at Psalm 13 so you can see the connection between lament and trust. This particular psalm contains only six verses, which makes it easy to memorize and examine.

Laments are designed to lead us toward decisive, faith-filled worship. We see this develop quickly in Psalm 13 as David combines his address and complaint to God in four *how long* questions. They are pointed and direct:

> How long, O Lord? Will you forget me forever?
> How long will you hide your face from me?
> How long must I take counsel in my soul
> and have sorrow in my heart all the day?
> How long shall my enemy be exalted over me? (vv. 1–2)

The next two verses feature David's request. He boldly asks for deliverance:

> Consider and answer me, O Lord my God; . . .
> lest I sleep the sleep of death. (13:3–4)

This lament follows a pattern that is hopefully now more familiar to you—from turning, to complaining, to asking. I hope you are starting to identify this framework in other psalms. But even more, I hope this pattern is starting to become your own prayer language.

But God . . .

In Psalm 13:5 David turns to a series of trust-laden statements that are rooted in the character of God. The shift starts with the word *but*.

> But I have trusted in your steadfast love;
>> my heart shall rejoice in your salvation.

In lament psalms the word *but* marks a critical and consistent turn toward trust. Michael Jinkins suggests that words such as *but* and *however* are found in every lament because lamenting trust is not merely a belief or conviction; it is trusting despite what circumstances might lead one to believe.[8] Words like *but*, *however*, and *yet* mark the intentional shift from the cause of the lament to trusting in who God is, what he has done, and the promises of Scripture.[9] Here are a few examples outside of Psalm 13:

> I have been forgotten like one who is dead;
>> I have become like a broken vessel. . . .

> *But* I trust in you, O LORD;
>> I say, "You are my God." (Ps. 31:12, 14)

> For my enemies speak concerning me;
>> those who watch for my life consult together
> and say, "God has forsaken him;
>> pursue and seize him,
>> for there is none to deliver him."

---

8. Michael Jinkins, *In the House of the Lord: Inhabiting the Psalms of Lament* (Collegeville, MN: Liturgical, 1989), 84.

9. I've compiled a list of other psalms illustrating the use (mainly) of *but* in appendix 4.

. . . *But* I will hope continually
    and will praise you yet more and more.
        (Ps. 71:10–11, 14)

O God, insolent men have risen up against me;
    a band of ruthless men seeks my life,
    and they do not set you before them.
But you, O Lord, are a God merciful and gracious,
    slow to anger and abounding in steadfast love and
        faithfulness. (Ps. 86:14–15)

Trust is believing what you know to be true even though the facts of suffering might call that belief into question. Lament keeps us turning toward trust by giving us language to step into the wilderness between our painful reality and our hopeful longings.

Three Affirmations of Trust

Psalm 13 makes this decisive turn with three affirmations in verses 5–6:

But I have trusted in your steadfast love;
    my heart shall rejoice in your salvation.
I will sing to the LORD,
    because he has dealt bountifully with me.

I hope these will become more than just words in your Bible. My desire is that you will pray them as well, helping your own heart to turn toward trust. These three affirmations are instructive. They help us know how to bring our laments to their completion.

1. *"I have trusted in your steadfast love."* God has a history with his people. He is trust-worthy. His people choose to trust him. That's the nature of the relationship, and the psalmist is

taking a historical look. As Jinkins notes, "The psalmist clings to trust in God's steadfast love on the basis of what God has done in the past, a confidence that made it possible to pray in the first place."[10] In the same way that it takes faith to turn to God in prayer while in pain, it takes faith to trust in God's steadfast love when circumstances are hard. This statement of trust anticipates a praise that has not yet arrived.[11] David connects his painful experience to what he knows to be true regarding God's covenantal love.

Every Christian has a record of God's steadfast love. Therefore, we should remind ourselves about God's worthiness to be trusted. To be a Christian means trusting in what God says and who he is. We came to faith that way. We trusted that the Bible is true. We believed forgiveness is possible for those who receive Christ. Trusting in God's grace welcomed us into God's family. But that was only the beginning.

Christians don't leave behind trusting God after coming to faith. On the contrary, being a follower of Jesus requires that we walk through life in continual trust. Seasons of suffering are no different. They are just harder and more intense. The stakes are higher and the emotions more raw. But trusting is still how we live.

If you picked up this book because you are searching for answers, you probably knew trust was the goal. Maybe you wondered, *How do I make it through this and trust God?* While there are no easy answers, I've found it helpful to echo the words of verse 5. As I personalize "I have trusted in your steadfast love," it reminds me of God's track record of faithfulness in my life. Sometimes I've prayed the same phrase over and over—almost like a chant. At other times I've prayed through

---

10. Jinkins, *In the House of the Lord*, 86.
11. Jinkins, *In the House of the Lord*, 86.

a list of all the ways God has been faithful. Or I rehearse the gospel, thanking God for life-changing truths like Galatians 2:20: "I have been crucified with Christ. It is no longer I who live, but Christ who lives in me. And the life I now live in the flesh I live by faith in the Son of God, who loved me and gave himself for me."

Choosing to trust requires reinforcing what we know to be true. Prayers of lament are designed to remind us that God is worthy to be trusted—even in this!

2. *"My heart shall rejoice in your salvation."* The second confident statement in Psalm 13:5 connects trust to rejoicing in God's plan of redemption. Time and time again God rescues his people. Suffering does not mean that God has forgotten or rejected his people. Rather, the long arc of God's plan for salvation is always at work—even though we cannot fully see the trajectory. A verse in Cowper's hymn gets to the heart of this issue:

> Blind unbelief is sure to err,
>   And scan his work in vain.
> God is his own interpreter,
>   And he will make it plain![12]

Choosing to trust through lament requires that we rejoice without knowing how all the dots connect. We decide to let God be his own interpreter, trusting that somehow his gracious plan is being worked out—even if we can't see it.

On this side of the cross we have a real advantage we need to embrace. We know that the ultimate lament cry—"My God, My God, why have you forsaken me?" (Ps. 22:1)—led to the greatest moment of redemption. The darkness of the sixth hour

---

12. Stebbing, *Poetical Works of William Cowper*, 405.

led to the dawn of the empty tomb. Jesus's life of lament led to salvation and eternal life. We know the full story of salvation.

In Romans 8 the apostle Paul applies this to hardship by wrapping suffering in the promises of God's redemptive plan. He lists the trials that Christians face: "Who shall separate us from the love of Christ? Shall tribulation, or distress, or persecution, or famine, or nakedness, or danger, or sword?" (Rom. 8:35). And then he quotes the complaint of a lament psalm:

> Yet for your sake we are killed all the day long;
>   we are regarded as sheep to be slaughtered.
>   (Ps. 44:22)

On either side of the trials and lament stand sweeping promises connected to God's eternal plan. In other words, promises don't end the pain, but they do give it purpose.

> And we know that for those who love God all things work together for good, for those who are called according to his purpose. (Rom. 8:28)

> What then shall we say to these things? If God is for us, who can be against us? (Rom. 8:31)

> No, in all these things we are more than conquerors through him who loved us. For I am sure that neither death nor life, nor angels nor rulers, nor things present nor things to come, nor powers, nor height nor depth, nor anything else in all creation, will be able to separate us from the love of God in Christ Jesus our Lord. (Rom. 8:37–39)

Paul rejoices in salvation. He takes the reality of suffering and the pain of lament, and combines them to highlight the glory and promise of God's love. This is what choosing to trust can do for you if you'll enter into it.

Lament calls us to point our hearts Godward by rejoicing in God's grace.

While I was writing this chapter, I preached at a funeral for a man named Terry. He and his wife became friends of ours over the years. Terry was the kind of man whose face seemed to be imprinted with a smile. He hugged everyone. He embodied what it means to be a joyful servant. His death was unexpected. The funeral was packed.

I preached on the lament in Romans 8, connecting the grief of the apostle Paul to the tragic groaning we all felt: another beloved husband, father, and friend was gone. While we celebrated some great memories about Terry, I reminded the congregation that there is something tragically wrong with funerals. I shared that they awaken us to the reality of the brokenness of the world in which we live. I was blunt about the fact that I'd really like my friend Terry to still be alive, and I hated the presence of death in the world.

While grief never left the room, we wrapped the hope of the gospel around our grief. I shared the sovereign and eternal promises connected to the lament of Romans 8 in order to help everyone understand that our grief was bookended in the promises and hope of salvation through Jesus. In other words, Terry's death was not the final word. We rejoiced in God's plan while grieving. And we even put into practice what the psalmist commends in the final verse of Psalm 13: we sang. As our protest against the presence of death in the world, we lifted our voices together and confessed our trust in God. We rejoiced in our salvation.

Entering lament leads to rejoicing.

3. *"I will sing to the* Lord, / *because he has dealt bountifully with me."* Verse 6 is the final statement of trust in Psalm 13. In this short psalm, notice that we've moved from pointed

questions to God-centered worship. As David allows lament to reorient his heart, he makes the choice to praise God for his grace and mercy. David's complaints and requests have now reached their intended destination: faith-filled worship.

The book of Job shows us the same progression. Job's innocent suffering and his unhelpful friends led him to a series of complaints. God answered Job out of the whirlwind in chapters 38–41 with a series of questions designed to show him God's breathtaking majesty and power. Job was left nearly speechless. Here are his own words:

> I know that you can do all things,
>   and that no purpose of yours can be thwarted. . . .
> I had heard of you by the hearing of the ear,
>   but now my eye sees you. (Job 42:2, 5)

The entire book of Job is designed not only to highlight innocent suffering but also to demonstrate that human questions and complaints eventually end in humble worship.

Other lament psalms connect trust, singing, and worship together as well. Two examples:

> The LORD is my strength and my shield;
>   in him my heart trusts, and I am helped;
> my heart exults,
>   and with my song I give thanks to him. (Ps. 28:7)

> You have kept count of my tossings;
>   put my tears in your bottle.
>   Are they not in your book?
> Then my enemies will turn back
>   in the day when I call.
>   This I know, that God is for me.
> In God, whose word I praise,
>   in the LORD, whose word I praise,

in God I trust; I shall not be afraid.
What can man do to me? (Ps. 56:8–11)

Throughout the psalms of lament there is this consistent destination of trust. Through all the pain, the questions, the unfair treatment at the hands of others, and the injustice, lament leads us to a place of worship. Todd Billings cites Augustine's helpful summary of how lament psalms, like all psalms, teach us to trust: "The psalms are given to us as a divine pedagogy for our affections—God's way of reshaping our desires and perceptions so that they learn to lament in the right things and take joy in the right things."[13]

Lament tunes the heart so it can sing about trust.

Varied Expressions of Trust

This destination of faith-filled worship takes different paths, depending on the circumstances and the state of your soul. Some days trust may sound like confident statements regarding what you know to be true about God as you meditate on some divine attribute. You might say, "God, I know you are in control. I do trust you." Other days you might simply rehearse the promises in the Word, especially at the end of the lament psalms. They tell you what to say. Echo their confidence.

Lament prayers could also end by quietly singing a song that captures what is true as we tune our hearts toward belief. A good hymnal or a sheet of choruses can be a great encouragement for your confidence in God. When we are battling falsehoods in our thinking, sometimes singing has the power to convince our emotions to change. Or you may find there

---

13. Todd Billings, *Rejoicing in Lament: Wrestling with Incurable Cancer and Life in Christ* (Grand Rapids, MI: Brazos, 2015), 38, citing Brian Brock, "Augustine's Incitement to Lament, from the *Enarrationes in Psalmos*," in *Evoking Lament: A Theological Discussion*, ed. Brian Brock and Eva Harasta (London: T&T Clark, 2009), 183–203.

are moments when you just need to sit quietly before the Lord. Exhaustion or weariness can create a silent language of trust. We can bank our confidence in this: "Be still and know that I am God" (Ps. 46:10).

Lament leads to trust, but the path is not always clear or straightforward. By turning to prayer, laying out our complaints, and boldly asking, we are brought by God to a place of growing trust in him.

Lament creates a path through the messy wilderness of pain.

Don't get hung up getting it perfect. You might start out by simply ending your prayer with "God, I choose to trust you today." That's it. That may be as much as you can muster. And that would be progress—a good first step. Or maybe, like me, you need the well-worn path of the psalms of lament as you make the prayer of Scripture your own. Allow your prayer to be the echo of ancient and inspired words. Think of how many hurting people have joined you in that chorus! Perhaps you could pick a song or hymn or a poem that will put words in your mouth and affection in your soul.

But whatever you do, don't stop making this turn toward trust. Learn to live in the tension of pain beyond belief and divine sovereignty beyond comprehension by stepping into trust. Choose to place your confidence in God. Learning to lament is a journey as we discover how lament can provide mercy when dark clouds loom. Lament is how you live between a hard life and God's promises. It is how we learn to sing and worship when suffering comes our way.

Though no one taught you how to cry, the steps of lament must be learned. It is vital to the Christian faith. It is how we make our way through the pains of life while clinging to the hope of the gospel. To lament is Christian as we turn to God in prayer, lay out our complaints, ask boldly, and choose to trust.

Trust the One Who Keeps You Trusting

While lament is a journey, the wonderful news is that you don't walk this path in your own strength. It's not simply a matter of your grit and willpower. Instead, God helps you to keep trusting him. He helps your lamenting.

In the week after the funeral of Sylvia, my brother-in-law, Rich, sent an email to John Piper about our devastating loss. Dr. Piper's books and sermons had been instrumental in the formation of my understanding of suffering and God's sovereignty. Rich asked if Dr. Piper might send me a short note of encouragement. The request somehow made it through the hundreds of emails he received. I remember the moment I saw a message pop up in my inbox with his name. It referenced that he had heard about the loss of our daughter and that he was praying for my wife and me through our terrible pain. After a few encouraging words, he closed with a statement that has become an anchor for my soul and often my target in lament: "Keep trusting the One who keeps you trusting."

This is how lament has served me and countless other believers. Tear-filled prayers, wrestling through tough questions, and banking my life on the promises of God are all part of the journey to keep me trusting. Learning to lament leads to trust.

Laments pivot on God's promises.[14]

I don't know how many times I've concluded a lament prayer by simply saying, "Lord, I'm trusting you to keep me trusting." And that is where God designed lament to lead. Through turning to God in prayer, laying out our complaints, and asking boldly for God's help, we are led to place our trust in a God who cares for us and hears us.

Learning to lament gives us the grace to keep trusting.

---

14. Billings, *Rejoicing in Lament*, 13.

Reflection Questions

1. What happens to the soul of someone who never moves to this last step of trust?

2. How do you think complaint and request set the framework for trust?

3. In your own words, how would you define trust? What are its ingredients? What does it sound like? Look like?

4. Why it is important to think about trust as "active patience"?

5. What are some barriers that can stand in your way of turning to trust?

6. Develop a list of your "go-to" promises, psalms, or songs. Write them down, and then share them with someone.

7. Before moving on to the next chapter, take some time to talk to the Lord about your need to trust him.

PART 2

LEARNING FROM LAMENT

LAMENTATIONS

5

A Broken World and a Holy God

Lamentations 1–2

The heart of the wise is in the house of mourning.

Ecclesiastes 7:4

Having learned how to lament through the Psalms, we are ready to consider what lament teaches us. We not only need to learn *to* lament; we also need to learn *from* lament. You may have picked up this book eager to learn how to process your pain or grief. I'm glad you've taken that step. Hopefully, part 1 helped you understand the progression of turning, complaining, asking, and trusting.

But there is another way lament can help you. It allows you to hear the lessons God intends to teach you through pain. C. S. Lewis famously said, "God whispers to us in our pleasures, speaks in our conscience, but shouts in our pains: it is

His megaphone to rouse a deaf world."[1] Suffering—at every level—is an opportunity to learn. However, we must be willing to listen. As Nicholas Wolterstorff says in his book *Lament for a Son*: "I shall look at the world through tears. Perhaps I shall see things that dry-eyed I could not see."[2] Lament can be a prism through which we see a path for growth.

In part 2 we will explore the book of Lamentations. Our aim is to walk through this historic lament to see what we can learn. The songs of sorrow in the Bible were more than expressions of personal grief. They were designed to help God's people never forget the lessons birthed out of pain or a crisis. Like the Vietnam Memorial with its dark granite walls and thousands of names, Lamentations beckons readers into a historical lament to learn important lessons—the kind that should be remembered.

Lament is not merely an expression of sorrow; it is a memorial.

An elderly man passed away after a grueling battle with Alzheimer's disease. His struggle took its toll on the family as they watched his memory fade, listened to repetitive sentences, and offered awkward reminders of one another's names. They walked through the slow sunset of a man they dearly loved.

One of our pastors opened the funeral service in a way that moved me. He spoke as a man who knew how to lament, and in fact, he did. His words were born out of the crucible of caring for his aging mother in her slow process of dying. It gave him a unique message:

> The reason we are here today is to open our souls to the ravages of emotions that a funeral brings. There is a right

---

1. C. S. Lewis, *The Problem of Pain* (New York: Collier, 1962), 93.
2. Nicolas Wolterstorff, *Lament for a Son* (Grand Rapids, MI: Eerdmans, 1987), loc. 127 of 562, Kindle.

way to lament and respond to the sorrow. There's a sense of relief at one level that your husband, father, and grandpa doesn't have to live with the affliction of memory loss, confusion, and frailty. Nor do the families and friends have to watch him go through this anymore. Because of the gospel there is a hope of expectation that life's final chapter has not been written. For the next hour we will open ourselves to overwhelming sorrow in the face of death, the quiet relief, and the glimmer of hope on the horizon.

The other reason we are here today is because "the heart of the wise is in the house of mourning." Make no mistake friends, this house that we are in today is a house of mourning. We should feel the stunning reality that a human being is no longer with us. A husband is gone. A father is gone. A grandfather is gone.

The merry-go-round of our lives has stopped, and we are forced to take a long look at death in the house of mourning. And wisdom can be ours as we face the realities of death and as we listen to the voice of God in this room through his Word.[3]

The funeral homily was a fitting reminder that death is shocking—even outrageous. The words were a candid protest that something is wrong with the world. The funeral became more than an expression of grief. It served as a reorientation to the brokenness that lies underneath all of our lives.

Lament is a place to learn.

Shock and Awe

While there are other places in the Bible where lament appears, the book of Lamentations is the most intense and comprehensive minor-key song in the Scriptures. It complains, weeps,

---

3. Funeral homily by Pastor Dale Shaw, September 4, 2015. Used by permission.

struggles, hopes, remembers, and clings. It reminds us who we are, who God is, and how brokenness is woven into the fabric of our world. It can awaken us to circumstances that should break our hearts. Through the chaos, Lamentations can become our teacher. It is a book of shock and awe.

As a pastor, I've had a front-row seat to significant grief and tragedy. Those moments are not only sad; they're instructive. I've left funerals contemplating how I long for death to be defeated, how much brokenness there is in the world, how quickly time passes, and how grateful I am for the resurrection of Jesus. What's more, I've found myself savoring a family meal more deeply, saying goodnight to my kids with greater meaning, hugging my wife a little longer, or reading my Bible more slowly because I've been to the house of mourning.

Lament can retune our hearts to what's really important. It can invite us to consider what lies underneath our lives—what really matters. That is why Christians should be familiar with lament and the book of Lamentations. Those who know the biblical plan of creation-fall-redemption-restoration should be able to walk through moments of sorrow while connecting everything to the bigger story of the holiness of God and the hope of the gospel.

Never Forget

Before we dive into the first two chapters of Lamentations, it's important you understand the background of the book. Lamentations was written by the prophet Jeremiah to reflect upon the destruction of Jerusalem in 586 BC. He wanted generations to never forget the lessons from this dark moment in Israel's history.

After the reigns of Kings David and Solomon, the golden years of Israel, the nation was divided into two kingdoms. The northern kingdom was called Israel, and the southern kingdom, Judah. The northern kingdom was led by one wicked king after another. After ignoring repeated warnings from many prophets to turn back to God, Israel was conquered by Assyria in 722 BC. The defeat and captivity of the northern tribes should have warned the southern kingdom. But Judah eventually followed the same path of spiritual rebellion. The land was filled with idolatry, injustice, immorality, and corruption.

During this time, Babylon staged a three-year siege of Jerusalem, the capital city of the southern kingdom. The people nearly starved to death. Eventually, the city wall was breached. The Babylonian army sacked the capital, burned the temple, and tore down the walls surrounding the city of David. Everything of value was taken to Babylon. Those who survived the invasion became exiles and slaves. The glorious temple and the city were smoldering ruins.

Like the psalms of lament, the book of Lamentations is a collection of poems. The first two chapters introduce the theme of the book, and Lamentations reaches its climax in chapter 3. Chapters 4 and 5 do not conclude with a "rosy picture." Instead, Lamentations ends with pain still lingering and the city still in ruins. It does not resolve in a neat or tidy manner.

The structure of the book is also significant. Chapters 1 and 2 were written as an acrostic. The first letter of each verse is a successive character of the Hebrew alphabet.[4] This form is designed to emphasize the comprehensive nature of Jerusalem's destruction. Jeremiah, the author, wants us to see suffering from A to Z. Again, this book is more than just a historical record.

As is the case with every lament, there is a history behind what's written in Lamentations. Much like the struggles that

---

4. F. B. Huey, *Jeremiah, Lamentations*, The New American Commentary (Nashville: Broadman & Holman, 1993), 445.

are a part of your story, the circumstances of life are the canvas on which God paints a picture. There's a narrative through every person's life. Whether it's the story of Judah's fall or the perplexing elements of your life, there are lessons to be learned. Lament not only vocalizes the pain but can also memorialize the message beneath the struggle—if we'll listen and not forget.

Lamentations 1–2: A Broken World and a Holy God

The first word of chapters 1 and 2 reflects the tone of the entire book. In English it is translated as "How." It can be read as both an expression of shock and a question.

> How lonely sits the city
> that was full of people! (Lam. 1:1)

> How the Lord in his anger
> has set the daughter of Zion under a cloud! (Lam. 2:1)

In the original Hebrew, "How?" is the title of the book.[5] It reflects the struggle of this lament: How could this happen? How can God allow this? How can God's people survive? How do we think about the future? These are the questions you ask when facing the dark clouds of grief. These are the questions and complaints of lament.

The first two chapters lead with this shocking sorrow. Jerusalem is portrayed as a broken, lonely widow and a princess now a slave (Lam. 1:1). The city weeps with "tears on her cheeks," being abandoned by her former lovers and opposed by friends (1:2). The once-glorious nation is now scattered "among the nations" with no resting place (1:3). She has been overrun by her adversaries.

---

5. R. K. Harrison, *Jeremiah and Lamentations: An Introduction and Commentary*, Tyndale Old Testament Commentaries (Downers Grove, IL: InterVarsity Press, 1973), 197.

Central to the pain is the triumph of the enemy. God didn't intervene. Lamentations 1:5 goes further, saying "her enemies prosper." The blessing of the Lord seems to have been given to the enemies of God's people. Lamentations, like all laments, gives us language to wonder—out loud—*How did this happen?*

But this book presses suffering even further, highlighting the cause behind the grief. It says "because the LORD has afflicted her" (Lam. 1:5). Jeremiah has no problem identifying that while Babylon was the means, God was ultimately orchestrating the destruction of Jerusalem.

Lamentations awakens us to a broken world and a holy God. The second chapter of Lamentations expands on this theme:

> The Lord has swallowed up without mercy
>   all the habitations of Jacob;
> in his wrath he has broken down
>   the strongholds of the daughter of Judah;
> he has brought down to the ground in dishonor
>   the kingdom and its rulers.
>
> He has cut down in fierce anger
>   all the might of Israel;
> he has withdrawn from them his right hand
>   in the face of the enemy;
> he has burned like a flaming fire in Jacob,
>   consuming all around. (Lam. 2:2–3)

There is a great tension here connected to the presence of pain and the sovereignty of God. However, it is left unresolved. Many questions remain unanswered. While the city smolders, one thought dominates: "How!"

I'm sure you can relate to this. Life is full of vexing questions related to God's purposes. Pain often highlights perplexing paradoxes. Lament is expressed even though the tension remains. It turns to God in prayer, vocalizes the complaint, asks boldly, and chooses to trust while uncertainty hangs in the air. Lament doesn't wait for resolution. It gives voice to the tough questions before the final chapter is written.

Lament is a journey through the shock and awe of pain.

Broken by Sin

The picture in the first two chapters of Lamentations is not pretty. The destruction of the city, its culture, and its people is disturbing, but Lamentations is not silent as to why it happened. Jeremiah laments:

> Her foes have become the head;
>   her enemies prosper,
> because the LORD has afflicted her
>   for the multitude of her transgressions. (Lam. 1:5)

> Jerusalem sinned grievously. (Lam. 1:8)

> Your prophets have seen for you
>   false and deceptive visions;
> they have not exposed your iniquity
>   to restore your fortunes,
> but have seen for you oracles
>   that are false and misleading. (Lam. 2:14)

The message is clear: the people are facing the judgment of God because of their sin.

Despite being God's chosen people and the object of his covenantal love, the kingdom of Judah reached a point where the scales of divine justice tipped. God leveled his own temple. He scattered his own people. He ruined his own city. Judah believed they could do whatever they wanted with God's commandments. They were dismissive of God's rule in their life. It led to this moment.

Their sinfulness led to their brokenness. The cause of this destruction is central to the message of Lamentations. While God values his people, there is something more important than the preservation of the city: God's righteousness. Therefore, Lamentations mourns over more than the destruction of Jerusalem. It laments the problem that lies underneath—the sinfulness of the nation. The people abandoned God in their worship, their actions, and even their hearts.

What happened to Jerusalem is an important example of the devastation sin always creates. Poetically, it sounds like this:

> . . . she became filthy;
> all who honored her despise her,
>   for they have seen her nakedness;
> she herself groans
>   and turns her face away.
>
> Her uncleanness was in her skirts;
>   she took no thought of her future;
> therefore her fall is terrible. (Lam.1:8–9)

The language is full of shame.

The issue is compounded by the fact that sin has affected an entire nation. The scale of waywardness and devastation makes this scene horrific. The sanctuary has been defiled by other nations; all the people groan as they search for bread (Lam. 1:10–11). According to chapter 2, their leaders were taken captive. There is no access to the Law. The prophets have no word from the Lord. The elders are silent and in mourning. And the young women are weeping (Lam. 2:10). Everywhere you look there is devastation. Brokenness.

The depth of the destruction is shocking.

This reminds me of a time I visited Auschwitz and Birkenau. It was the first time I fully understood the depth and scale of human depravity. Auschwitz is a relatively small compound in the middle of the city that bears its name. It is now converted into a haunting museum featuring the depravity of the Jewish genocide in World War II. Walking through buildings that resemble a small college, you get a sense of the methodical and demented crimes committed there. There are rooms full of shoes, luggage, and human hair. Other buildings feature descriptions of perverse experiments and pictures of men, women, and children who died there. Auschwitz is sickening.

Outside the city is Birkenau—another camp. It is incomprehensible. The compound is 425 acres with over three hundred buildings.[6] The scale of depravity is shocking. I walked Birkenau for hours. As far as I looked, I could see the remaining brick chimneys from the barracks spread over the green fields. I walked inside the ruins of a gas chamber and near a field of mass graves. Historians estimate that over a million people were killed in these two camps.

Auschwitz/Birkenau showed me, firsthand, the scale of human depravity. I knew that sin was destructive, but the scope of what I saw deepened my understanding of how heinous sin could be. I'll never forget this shocking experience. It marked me for life.

Memorials help us remember by making us feel the weight of a tragedy. Without them, we are prone to forget and repeat the mistakes of the past. They remind us that there are lessons to be learned. The smoldering ruins of Jerusalem sent a message, and Lamentations is its memorial. The lesson is clear: God is long-suffering and merciful, but rebellion against his rule has

6. Michael Berenbaum, "Auschwitz," Encyclopaedia Britannica, August 22, 2018, https://www.britannica.com/place/Auschwitz.

consequences. Lamentations was written to mourn the scale of the brokenness in the world. The fall of Jerusalem reminds us of the powerful nature of sin and the sacredness of God's holiness. Sin is that bad, and God is that holy.

Lamentations is a memorial to a broken world and a holy God.

A Turning to God

In the closing verses of chapter 1, Jeremiah pleads for mercy. After rehearsing the facts of what happened to the people of God, he offers a confession:

> The LORD is in the right,
>> for I have rebelled against his word. (Lam. 1:18)

Jeremiah draws a straight line from their rebellion to their suffering. He gives it more color in verse 19:

> I called to my lovers,
>> but they deceived me.

There is no doubt in his mind as to the connection between the people's suffering and their spiritual adultery. God warned them, and now he has their attention. The shocking language, the emotional imagery, and the wrestling with divine purposes are all designed to tune our hearts to hear something we often need: a spiritual wake-up call.

Lament is the song we sing while living in a world that is under the curse of sin. Lament longs for the day when cities like Jerusalem will no longer be leveled. Just think of it—there will be no lament in the New Jerusalem. Revelation 21 makes this stunning promise: "He will wipe away every tear from their eyes, and death shall be no more, neither shall there be mourning, nor crying, nor pain anymore, for the former things have passed away" (Rev. 21:4). But in the meantime, this minor-key song shines a light on the brokenness underneath our human experience.

In the same way funerals stop the "merry-go-round" of life, laments invite us to consider lessons emerging from the rubble. A broken world will bring its share of grief, but it can also bring wisdom if we are willing to slow down, listen, and learn. Lament is an uncomfortable yet helpful teacher. It is true: "The heart of the wise is in the house of mourning" (Eccles. 7:4).

The Wisdom of Lamentations

What might we learn from these opening chapters of Lamentations? What can lament teach us? Let me suggest three potential lessons emerging from the first two chapters.

Sin Is the Real Problem

All lament and suffering have their roots in the fallen state of the world. Sorrow and pain owe their beginning to rebellion against God's reign. Lament interprets all suffering through the lens of the Bible's understanding of the problem of sin in the world.

Now, I'm not suggesting that *every* negative circumstance or *all* suffering you experience is directly connected to a specific sin in your life. To be clear: I'm not saying that *every* painful calamity is a result of your or my bad choices. Sometimes bad choices are the problem, and God lovingly allows the consequences of our sinful actions to bear their ugly fruit—"The Lord disciplines the one he loves" (Heb. 12:6). But we have to be careful not to over-apply the situation in Lamentations.

At the same time, I don't want to ignore an important caution. While not every suffering may be connected directly to specific sin in your life, it would be a mistake to diminish the connection between the fallen state of the world and pain. The Bible tells us that God is holy and mankind has fallen short of his glory (Rom. 3:23). The result of this sinful rebellion is death (Rom. 6:23). The effect of our collective treason is the groaning of creation under this brokenness (Rom. 8:22). We, along with the entire created order, long for a better day (Rom. 8:23). Therefore, a Christian should understand that beneath every painful aspect of our humanity is the reality of sin. Every death, every war, every injustice, every loss, every hurt, and every tear owe their existence to sin. It has affected everything. Lamentations reminds us that underlying our lives is a foundational brokenness connected to the presence of sin in the world.

Without sin there would be no lament.

As I was writing this chapter, my eleven-year-old daughter approached me with a sad look on her face. She had been walking along the side of our house, and she noticed a little stone in a flower garden with our stillborn daughter's name on it. She asked, "Dad, why did Sylvia have to die?" Her question was preciously blunt. Who doesn't wrestle with a question like this?

Here's what I said. Take note of the last two sentences: "Savannah, we don't know why the Lord decided to take Sylvia. His plans are mysterious. But we know the Bible says all his ways are for our good. So, there's a really good reason, and we'll know it someday. For now, we can trust him. But also, Sylvia died because we live in a fallen world affected by sin. Her death and our sadness remind us that we need Jesus to come and make everything right."

This is not the first time I've given someone this answer. Funerals and laments remind us that sin is serious. Sorrow points us to somber realities—about God, about us, and about our need for a Savior. Underneath the destruction of Jerusalem, every pain, and all our laments is the real problem: sin.

My Sin and Suffering Are Not the Only Problems

Our natural bias is to individualize suffering. We might ask questions like "Why is this happening to *me*? What did *I* do to deserve this?" Pain can make a person rather self-focused. Additionally, it's far too easy to keep the pain of others at a distance. I typically feel little emotion for tragedies that do not affect me directly. I need to be reminded that my pain is not the only pain.

These first two chapters of Lamentations remind us that sin is far more sweeping than just our individual experience. Our collective rebellion against God surfaces in our culture, families, cities, and nations. There are systemic problems within the fabric of our humanity that can be traced to a fundamental brokenness in the world. Minor-key prayers remind us that brokenness has made its way in every part of humanity.

I hope this book helps you to pray lament-oriented prayers not only for your own pain but also for the pain of others near you. My aim is that God would give you a bigger heart for what is wrong with your neighborhood, your city, your nation, and your world, not just what's wrong with your life.

More than just providing comfort and help in our times of sorrow, the grace of lament helps tune our hearts to the pain of others and to the foundational truths about God and the world. We can lament on behalf of our culture, identifying with the brokenness around us. When leaders fall, scandals shock, or unrighteousness reigns, we have a prayer language to embrace the disappointment instead of casting judgment. I recently heard Mark Dever say, "We watch the news so we know how to pray."[7] So true. But perhaps we could also say, "We watch the news so we know how to lament."

---

7. Phone conference with pastors, October 25, 2017.

I hope your heart will be awakened to hear the "groan" of the creation. Lament gives you eyes to see the brokenness around you.

Lament Awakens the Soul

Lament is one of the ways that a heart is tuned toward God's perspective. When the bottom drops out of your family, your culture, your city, or your nation, what do you say? If we are not careful, followers of Jesus can respond with fear, anger, or despair. In so doing we reveal a love affair with our culture. We can act as if we do not know the long arc of biblical history.

Rather than being angry, fearful, apathetic, or despairing, we should choose to lament. We can follow the example of the lament psalms, moving through complaint toward trust. And we should follow Jeremiah's example at the fall of Jerusalem. We should express our sorrow while allowing lament to reaffirm the important spiritual realities underlying our lives, our culture, and our future. God has a bigger plan. He can be trusted.

In this way, lament can awaken our souls from apathy. It can help us as we intentionally mourn the devastating effects of sin in our lives and the world. For example, when I was teaching on Lamentations at my church, I challenged our people to spend some time the following week mourning over the sin in their lives and in the world. One man took the challenge. He stopped me in the gym to share what was happening in his life. He said, "Mark, lament has given me a new ability to fight temptation!" He explained that he'd spent a significant amount of time that week lamenting the brokenness in the world and all the tragic effects of sin he could remember. Much to his surprise, lament lingered with him all day. He saw temptations through a new lens. He felt the weight of sin differently. He found it easier to win the battle with wrong desires because lament unmasked the empty promises. This minor-key song opened the door to a path of new freedom in his life.

Do you see now why it is better to go to the house of mourning? The book of Lamentations is in the Bible for a reason. We should allow it to awaken our hearts. There are lessons in lament that we can learn.

The first two chapters of Lamentations remind us that there is something wrong with the world. Lament has the potential to turn our hearts Godward as we sing in a minor key about our individual and corporate need for God's mercy. Lament reminds us that the problem in the world is sin, and God is the only one who can make it right.

In this respect, lament can be a welcomed wake-up call—a memorial—to the brokenness of the world and the holiness of God.

Reflection Questions

1. What were your impressions of the book of Lamentations before reading this chapter?
2. What lessons have you learned from "the house of mourning"?
3. List some examples of the brokenness around you or in you that have become too common and unnoticed.
4. What are some ways that lament can reorient your thinking about the world and yourself?
5. How would this reorientation affect your view of your own suffering or the suffering of others?
6. Do you agree that we tend to over-individualize suffering? Why is that the case? How does Lamentations help us to change that?
7. What are some practical steps—like confession—that you could take to allow lament to remind you what lies underneath our lives?

6

Hope Springs from Truth Rehearsed

Lamentations 3

> We may hear our hearts say, "It's hope-less!" but we should argue back.
>
> *Timothy Keller*

While attending a meeting at a Christian conference center, I noticed a picture on the wall. It featured a painted scene of a small English cottage tucked between two mountains with a flowing stream. A small garden surrounded the house. It resembled a Thomas Kinkade painting with pastel colors, soft lines, and a bright sky—the kind of art you'd find in a Christian bookstore. This soothing refuge would be a place I'd love to visit—one of peace and tranquility.

Below the painting was Lamentations 3:22–23:

> The steadfast love of the LORD never ceases;
>> his mercies never come to an end;
> they are new every morning;
>> great is your faithfulness.

The artist connected this famous verse to the idealized scene. I would guess many Christians would do the same.

But they'd be wrong.

A pastel-colored cottage by a stream is not the scene of the third chapter of Lamentations. On the contrary, Jeremiah writes "his mercies are new every morning" over a dark and tragic landscape. Instead of an English cottage, the city of Jerusalem lay in ruins. Think Indonesia after a tsunami, not a cabin in the Smokies. Bright skies are replaced with looming dark clouds. Quaint gardens are exchanged for streets of suffering. Instead of a peaceful scene, it's a war zone. Yet, as Jeremiah laments this destruction, he still says, "The steadfast love of the LORD never ceases."

That changes how we read Lamentations 3:22–23. Or at least it should. And it gives us a second lesson we can learn from lament.

Lamentation 3: Pointing the Heart to Truth

Jeremiah doesn't merely lament his pain and disappointment. He uses his song of sorrow to point his heart toward what he knows to be true despite what he sees. In effect, he says, "Even in the leveling of Jerusalem, God is still in control. Despite the destruction of Judah, his mercies never come to an end. God's faithfulness is still great."

This is where biblical lament is transformative. It not only gives voice to the pain you feel but also anchors your heart to truths you believe—or are trying to believe when dark clouds linger. Something bad may have happened in your life, which is why you are reading this book. Whatever the reason, loss can feel like a wasteland. It's devastating. But lament helps us to rehearse biblical truth so hope will return. Despite what you see, despite what you feel, despite what you think, lament can be a supply of grace as you affirm that God's mercies are new every day.

As you rehearse what is true, hope can rise. I promise. God promises too.

Two Different Perspectives in the Same Chapter

Everything in Lamentations builds to this point. Chapter 3 is the climax of the book. Here its acrostic structure changes. Instead of each verse starting with the next letter of the Hebrew alphabet, the same letter begins three verses before a new trio of verses features the subsequent letter, creating an intensified triplet acrostic.[1] This is the summit of the book.

Lamentations reaches its crescendo with two contrasting sections on hardship. The change in tone is dramatic. Let me illustrate this with two representative verses:

My endurance has perished,
    so has my hope from the LORD. (Lam. 3:18)

You have taken up my cause, O Lord;
    you have redeemed my life. (Lam. 3:58)

Do you see the clear contrast? The first part of Lamentations 3 (vv. 1–20) is dark and hopeless, while the second part (vv. 21–66) reflects an emerging level of trust. Let's explore this to see what we can learn.

"No Hope"

In Lamentations 3:18, Jeremiah sounds like he's given up: "It's over. There's no hope." Ever been there? I have. And I'm sure

---

1. R. K. Harrison, *Jeremiah and Lamentations: An Introduction and Commentary*, Tyndale Old Testament Commentaries (Downers Grove, IL: InterVarsity Press, 1973), 227.

you have too. There is an amplification of the pain he feels. In the first five verses we get a sense of his struggle:

> I am the man who has seen affliction
> > under the rod of his wrath;
> he has driven and brought me
> > into darkness without any light;
> surely against me he turns his hand
> > again and again the whole day long.
>
> He has made my flesh and my skin waste away;
> > he has broken my bones;
> he has besieged and enveloped me
> > with bitterness and tribulation. (Lam. 3:1–5)

The suffering has become personal and overwhelming. There seems to be no peace or happiness, no endurance or hope (Lam. 3:17–18). The grief of the moment is relentless. Jeremiah has reached the bottom.

This is one reason why I love Lamentations. Its gutsy honesty and emotional rawness are refreshing. I've lived what Jeremiah is feeling. I've felt the hopelessness of grief and the weary uncertainty of God's purposes. I've wrestled with God's plan. It helps me to know that I'm not alone in that struggle. I hope you feel the same.

Perhaps you picked up this book and read this far while thinking, *I've got no faith. I'm on empty. I'm not sure I can trust God anymore.* Lamentations 3:20 is for you:

> My soul continually remembers it [the affliction]
> > and is bowed down within me.

This verse is in the Bible for a reason. The good news is that if you're at the bottom, God can meet you there.

Lament is the language of those stumbling in their journey to find mercy in dark clouds.

"You Have Taken Up My Cause, O Lord!"

However, the perspective changes. As honest as Jeremiah is with his pain, he does not stay there. In the same way that the Psalms move us from complaint toward trust, Jeremiah embraces a completely different perspective. The city is still destroyed. The people are still in pain. But something has changed.

> I called on your name, O LORD,
>   from the depths of the pit;
> you heard my plea, "Do not close
>   your ear to my cry for help!"
> You came near when I called on you;
>   you said, "Do not fear!"
>
> You have taken up my cause, O Lord;
>   you have redeemed my life. (Lam. 3:55–58)

Do you hear the difference? There's still suffering and struggle, but the tone is different. That leads us to a critical question, one that is central to the spiritual value of lament: What changed? Or maybe the question is more personal for you: How can my perspective change?

Dare to Hope

Lamentations 3:21 is the key. It is what we learned by looking at the Psalms. Laments turn on words like *yet* and *but*. Here is what Jeremiah says:

> But this I call to mind,
>   and therefore I have hope. (Lam. 3:21)

In the New Living Translation, verse 21 reads,

> Yet I still *dare to hope*
>   when I remember this.

This helps us get to the heart of a valuable lesson. The destruction of Jerusalem sends a message, but it is not the entire story. The phrase "call to mind" (ESV) or "remember" (NLT) uses Hebrew words focused on the heart or the essence of one's being.[2] In other words, Jeremiah is drawing from the very center of what he believes. He uses his theology and what he believes as the basis for hope. He dares to hope again.

This is the pivot point in chapter 3 and the bridge between its two sections. It is the critical shift toward bold requests and choosing to trust that we learned through the lament psalms. On a personal level, this also could be a turning point for you. In fact, I hope once you see this, you'll embrace the value of lament as not only an expression of your heart but also something to help you think differently.

Lament dares to hope while life is hard.

As we put lament into practice and as we choose to rehearse what we believe, we learn to walk by faith. Connecting faith to lament in his book *Lament for a Son*, Nicolas Wolterstorff writes, "Faith is a footbridge that you don't know will hold you up over the chasm until you're forced to walk out onto it."[3]

Lament is a prayer of faith despite your fear.

I want you to learn from this shift in mind-set. Lamentations shows us that hope does not come from a change of circumstances. Rather, it comes from what you know to be true despite the situation in front of you. In other words, you live through suffering by what you believe, not by what you see or feel. While the circumstances of life have a narrative to them, there's

---

2. Andrew Bowling, "1071 לֵבָב," in *Theological Wordbook of the Old Testament*, ed. R. Laird Harris, Gleason L. Archer Jr., and Bruce K. Waltke (Chicago: Moody Press, 1999), 466.

3. Nicolas Wolterstorff, *Lament for a Son* (Grand Rapids, MI: Eerdmans, 1987), loc. 388 of 562, Kindle.

a biblical narrative underneath. Tim Keller, in his book *Walking with God through Pain and Suffering*, illustrates this for us:

> We may hear our hearts say, "It's hopeless!" but we should argue back. We should say, "Well, that depends what you were hoping in. Was that the right thing to put so much hope in?" Notice how the psalmist [in Psalm 42] analyzes his own hopes—"Why are you so cast down, O my soul?" Notice that he admonishes himself. "Put your hope in God, for I will yet praise him." The psalmist is talking to his heart telling it to go to God, looking to God.[4]

In the midst of the darkest moments of your life, I hope you'll have the courage and conviction to say: "But I call to mind what God is like. I'm going to rehearse what I know to be true. I'm going to recite what I know I believe. I'm going to dare to hope."

That fight isn't easy, though, is it? Believe me, I know. When the discouraging narrative in my own mind takes over, I have to fight to reorient my heart. I have to battle thoughts like *God doesn't love me. He is not going to take care of me. He's abandoned me. I'm alone. There's no way this could happen to me and God still care.*

You may be in that same place. You're reading this, thinking, *I don't know if I can do this anymore,* and yet you're here, reading. You're turning the pages, searching for hope. I'm here to tell you that God's Word says you can fight because you can call the promises of God to mind, and therefore, you can have hope. Lament can help you by rehearsing the truth of the Bible—to preach to your heart, to interpret pain through the lens of God's character and his ultimate mercy.

---

4. Timothy Keller, *Walking with God through Pain and Suffering* (New York: Riverhead, 2013), 289–90.

In our laments we express the sorrow we feel. But we also rehearse the truths we believe. We interpret pain through the lens of God's character and his ultimate mercy. By "calling to mind" important truths, we are able to stop listening to the circumstances around us and even the noise inside our heads.

Lament helps us to dare to hope again, and again, and again.

Hope Springs from Truth Rehearsed

In the middle of Lamentations 3 (vv. 22–33), are four truths upon which Jeremiah anchored his heart. The turning point for his soul was using lament to pour out his heart while, at the same time, daring to hope in what he knew to be true.

1. God's mercy never ends. Suffering of any kind may cause us to wonder if God is no longer merciful. But Lamentations 3:22–24 promises that God's love never ceases—even under dark clouds. Read these two verses slowly. They are rich and deeply comforting.

> The steadfast love of the LORD never ceases;
>> his mercies never come to an end;
> they are new every morning;
>> great is your faithfulness.
> "The LORD is my portion," says my soul,
>> "therefore I will hope in him."

Verse 22 uses an important Hebrew word for love: *hesed.* This is God's covenant love for his people. It is rooted in his character. It is the essence of who God is and how he relates to his people. All of God's actions are rooted in *hesed.* Therefore, the ultimate hope for God's people is God's ability to keep being God. But there's more.

According to verse 23 this mercy is new every morning. By "new," Jeremiah does not mean that these mercies never existed in the past. Rather, as Old Testament professor Duane Garrett describes it, Jeremiah means that in each new day, we see both evidence of God's grace and there is a possibility of renewal and repentance.[5] God supplies the mercy and grace we need every day. We endure because divine mercy is never exhausted.

That's a promise we must believe.

What's more, God's mercy leads us to himself. Verse 24 says,

> The LORD is my portion . . .
> therefore I will hope in him.

When God strips you of everything, and all you have is him, you have enough. Therefore, lament can awaken you to the truth of God's *hesed*. It can remind you that God is everything you really need.

Sometimes my last prayer of the day is a faith-filled, promise-claiming lament. I climb into bed exhausted because all day I've had to wrestle with my thinking. When sorrow and weariness try to take over the closing moments of my day, I pray something like this:

> Lord, I'm weary and tired. I'm discouraged, and I don't know how I'm going to do this again tomorrow. But I believe your mercies are going to be new when I wake up. I believe that I will never run out of your steadfast love. I'm trusting that you have enough grace for me for what I face. I'm going to sleep because I'm hoping in you.

In lament, we are honest with the struggles of life while also reminding ourselves that God never stops being God. His steadfast love never ends. He is sufficient. Therefore, our hope is not in a change of circumstances but in the promise of a God

---

5. Duane Garrett, *Song of Songs/Lamentations*, Word Biblical Commentary (Dallas: Word, 2004), 414–15.

who never stops being merciful—even when dark clouds loom. His mercy never ceases.

2. *Waiting is not a waste*. The second truth has become a personal favorite of mine over the last ten years because waiting for anything feels like a complete waste of time. Waiting for God to move or answer seems even worse. Lamentations 3:25–27 shows us the value of living in the space between suffering and restoration. Lament serves us well as we mourn and wait.

> The Lord is good to those who wait for him,
>   to the soul who seeks him.
> It is good that one should wait quietly
>   for the salvation of the Lord.
> It is good for a man that he bear
>   the yoke in his youth.

What you cannot see in your English translation is that verses 25–27 all begin with the Hebrew word "good."[6] It could read:

> Good is the Lord to those who wait for him,
> Good it is that one should wait quietly for the salvation of
>   the Lord,
> Good it is for a young man to bear the yoke in his youth.

So there is obviously something good here. What is it? To wait on the Lord means to place your hope in him—to trust that God is the one who can deliver you. Your entire confidence rests on him. We wait upon the Lord because he is God and we are not.

Why is waiting so difficult? Because it feels as if we're not doing anything. And that's the point. You're not doing anything, but God is. However, waiting is one of the greatest

6. F. B. Huey, *Jeremiah, Lamentations*, The New American Commentary (Nashville: Broadman & Holman, 1993), 474.

applications of the Christian faith. You are putting your trust in God, placing your hope in him, and expressing confidence that he is in control. Waiting puts us in an uncomfortable place where we're out of control of our lives. Remember in chapter 4, when I called this "active patience"? That season is when God will shape and define us the most.

However, I'm not saying waiting is easy. The uncertainty of what may or may not happen can be haunting. It can occupy too much space in our thinking. I've had it affect my sleep and assault my mind with the first thoughts of the day. Waiting can be hard because of the fear of what might happen. Our inability to do anything but wait is a powerless feeling. We want to know the answer. We want to know what's going on. We want to know, "What's the point of this? Why is this happening? Why is my life not like I want?"

Rather than resisting this season, we can see waiting as an opportunity for life-changing lessons. And that is one of the reasons why verse 27 says it's good for a man that he bear the yoke in his youth. To learn the value of waiting early in life would be a beautiful gift.

If you are in a position of waiting, let Lamentations remind you that waiting is not a waste. In your lament, why not release control of your life and say, "God, I don't know what you're doing or why, but I'm going to trust that you're God and I'm not." If God's providence requires you to wait, remind your heart that much good can come from this season. The Lord desires to teach us many lessons, and those lessons often come slowly—after we have stopped trying on our own, at the point we are broken and ready for him to lead us. In the midst of suffering, remember that waiting on the Lord is not a waste.

3. The final word has not been spoken. The third truth re-lates to our belief about the future. Suffering often involves the fear that it will never end or that it has no purpose. That is why the Bible is clear about suffering not being the final word. The biblical promises about God's purposes, his character, and the future are all designed to remind us that suffering and pain are not ultimately victorious.

Lament not only mourns the brokenness of suffering; it also looks expectantly toward what is yet to come. Lamentations 3:31–32 is filled with great hope and encouragement:

> For the Lord will not
> cast off forever,
> but, though he cause grief, he will have compassion
> according to the abundance of his steadfast love.

These verses assure us that all suffering has limits and purpose. They remind us that God's plan for us is full of compassion and an abundance of steadfast love. Everything is working out according to his loving plan for the believer's life.

At some point in the future, the final word will be spoken. God is going to intervene, and lament is one of the ways we defiantly say, "This is not over!" In fact, the pain that causes lament can create a longing for the future like nothing else. Maybe you need to put this book down and thank the Lord that "this is not over." Christians long for the day when faith shall be sight. Until then, we lament by faith.

One of my favorite places for lament is the cemetery where our stillborn daughter is buried. I will never forget the sense of profound loss as I placed a small casket in the cold ground in the middle of winter. Walking away from her graveside was one of the most painful things my wife and I ever experienced. You would think that with the painful memories connected to that location, I would never want to return. But it's actually the opposite.

Etched on Sylvia's grave marker are the words "Blessed be the name of the LORD," from Job 1:21. The words are a small protest against the tragedy of death. They are a memorial that even as we face death, we will bless the Lord. I have tearfully stood over that grave and said, "This is not over! One day Jesus is going to make this all right." So I love to return to that grave, because it is a constant reminder that not only has the Lord proven his compassion to me through the years of sorrow and pain, but there is also a coming day when graves will be emptied and death will be defeated.

Lament can point our hearts toward a future victory. Through the tears, we can still believe that the final word has not been spoken.

4. God is always good. The final truth is found in Lamentations 3:33:

> for he does not afflict from his heart
> > or grieve the children of men.

This text tells us that all of the destruction—the leveling of Jerusalem and the temple—does not come from a heart of God that enjoys his people's hardship.

God doesn't delight in the pain of his children. Rather, there are loving purposes behind every tear. You just can't see what they are yet. You don't know the whole story of what God is doing. In some cases there may be a day when you will be able to see the purposes of God. But usually things are not that clear. Instead, we have to simply trust that God is good. We have to believe his intentions are kind—that somehow pain and hardship are for our ultimate good. Rest assured that if you're a follower of Jesus, everything in your life is part of God's good purposes for you. He's not enjoying your struggle, but it's producing something in you that fits with God's good heart toward you. Lament can remind us that pain has a purpose. God is always good.

The anniversary date of Sylvia's death casts a shadow over our family. The date hits me differently every year. I have to go back to the truths found in these chapters. This year I wrote a poem to lament the agony and celebrate the triumph of God's grace in my life. It was a small way of anchoring my heart to the goodness of God yet again.

> This is the week when darkness loomed,
> as silence fell upon a womb;
> baby girl with beauty formed,
> nine months conceived, yet stillborn.
>
> A tiny casket, earth so cold.
> Graveside leaving, grief untold.
> Lingering sorrow, life that's scarred.
> Thirteen years and often hard.
>
> Through the years His promise, true:
> "I never will abandon you."
> Sustained by grace, my soul is filled,
> amazed he's kept me trusting still.
>
> My heart was crushed with grief not tame,
> but still in pain I believed The Name.
> My King has brought my faith to sight;
> He bought the right to make it right.
>
> And so in memory of loss
> I count it won and, by the cross,
> a little beat I longed to hear
> became a place where God drew near.
>
> Sovereign plan, mysterious,
> yet my path: "I choose to bless."

Hard is hard, hard's not bad;
clung to grace with all I've had.

An empty crib and painful date.
Death my foe, which I still hate.
But through it all I've seen the hand
of a loving God with a sovereign plan.

In lament we reaffirm what we believe. We say to ourselves, "God's mercy never ends," "waiting is not a waste," "the final word has not been spoken," and "God is always good."

In our fear and confusion, lament leads us back to what we know to be true: "Despite what I see, despite what I feel, God is good." Lament helps us to interpret pain through the lens of God's character and his ultimate mercy. The power of lament is the opportunity to express the sorrow we feel while also anchoring our hearts in the truth we believe. Lamentations 3 is one of the most compelling examples of this in the entire Bible. As the city of Jerusalem smolders, Jeremiah announces, "His mercies never come to an end." Lament is the language that moves us from our sorrow toward the truth of God's promises.

This minor-key song gives us courage to dare to hope again. When dark clouds linger, our laments can proclaim, "The steadfast love of the Lord never ceases."

Hope springs from truth rehearsed.

Reflection Questions

1. Prior to reading this chapter what was your perspective on Lamentations 3:22–23 or the song "Great Is Thy Faithfulness"? How has this chapter changed your understanding of the context of this text?

2. What comfort can we take from different perspectives on suffering in Lamentations 3?

3. Describe a time in your life when you would swing from "There's no hope" to "I can trust you, Lord!" What was that experience like?

4. Does the phrase "dare to hope" resonate with you? What is risky about hope when you are suffering?

5. Which of the four heart-shaping truths are most applicable to your life right now? Why?

6. In your own lament, what other truths do you need to rehearse? Take some time to write them down and pray over them.

7

Unearthing Idols

Lamentations 4

How the gold has grown dim,
   how the pure gold is changed!
The holy stones lie scattered
   at the head of every street.

Lamentations 4:1

On the morning of November 7, 2012, I felt like an exile.

And I didn't like it.

It was the day after the national election, and ballot initiatives sent a shocking message. Three states overwhelmingly approved the legalization of same-sex marriage. The people of Maryland, Maine, and Washington—from both coasts—affirmed a fundamental redefinition of marriage in the United States. Meanwhile, voters in Minnesota rejected a traditional marriage amendment to their constitution. What's more, two states approved the recreational use of marijuana. The moral tide in the United States had shifted. The election made that clear.

These issues were not new. But the rate of change was alarming.

Prior to this, I knew theoretically that the Bible called me an exile (1 Pet. 2:11). But as I watched the results and listened to the commentary that morning, I felt my exile status as never before. Al Mohler summarized the sentiment in a blogpost:

> Clearly, we face a new moral landscape in America. . . . We face a worldview challenge that is far greater than any political challenge, as we must learn how to winsomely convince Americans to share our moral convictions about marriage, sex, the sanctity of life, and a range of moral issues. This will not be easy.[1]

Unfortunately, I found Mohler's steady perspective to be rare among Christians in the weeks that followed. More frequently I found believers who were frightened, angry, or both. For some it was evident in their countenance. Some talked about being depressed. Others expressed blunt disgust with how politicians were ruining our country. In the weeks that followed, I received requests to mobilize our congregation toward political activism and lobbying—to save our country.

But that was just the beginning.

As other "culture wars" emerged over the next few years, I would see the same concerning pattern in fellow Christians as they came to grips with the uncoupling of Christianity from American culture. It became clear that my "exile awakening" was happening to a lot of other people. It was going to be a

---

1. Albert Mohler, "Aftermath: Lessons from the 2012 Election," Albert Mohler (blog), November 7, 2012, www.albertmohler.com/2012/11/07/aftermath-lessons-from -the-2012-election.

bumpy ride. Most Christians that I knew didn't know how to be exiles. They didn't want to be exiles.

Lament: Language of Exiles

Sensing this trend was one reason why I preached an eight-week series on the book of Lamentations. My pastor friends thought I was crazy for spending two months on such a dark subject. More than a few on our staff were nervous about how our church would respond. But our study proved to be one of the most fruitful seasons I remember.

As we walked through Lamentations, it gave us a language to express our struggles and fears. But it did something more. It helped us to see the world and ourselves through a different lens. As we dove deep into this book, lament helped uncover some hidden idols.

Lamentations mourns the effects of suffering on a society, but not simply because of the loss. It is a memorial to the futility of trusting in anything but God. It mourns the objects of trust that are common to any culture. In this way, the lament of Jeremiah can become a textbook of important lessons amid a culture in chaos.

Lament is the language that calls us, as exiles, to uncurl our fingers from our objects of trust.

Lamentations 4: Unearthing Idols

After seeing how a broken world and holy God are fundamental to our humanity and how hope can spring from truth rehearsed, we are going to learn how lament shines a spotlight on the things in which we place too much hope.

Think of your life as a beaker full of transparent liquid with sediment at the bottom.[2] If the beaker remains stable and still,

---

2. I'm grateful to John Piper for this illustration. I first heard it at a conference for pastors in 2005.

the solution looks clear—even pure. However, bump the beaker, and the sediment is activated. The appearance of purity is gone. Suffering bumps the beaker of our lives. It stirs up the sediments we forgot about or tried to hide. Fear, pride, covetousness, and self-sufficiency lie dormant. But pain can reveal these covert enemies.

Hardship reveals idols.

Why am I using the term "idols"? In the Bible an idol is simply an object of trust that takes the emotional and practical place of God. In the Old Testament, idolatry involved praying to the god of thunder or the goddess of fertility because of the belief that rain and the health of livestock were on the line. However, idolatry didn't end with the advent of the modern era. Timothy Keller, in his book *Counterfeit Gods*, provides a contemporary definition:

> What is an idol? It is anything more important to you than God, anything that absorbs your heart and imagination more than God, anything you seek to give you what only God can give. A counterfeit God is anything so central and essential to your life that, should you lose it, your life would feel hardly worth living.[3]

We worship idols—allow them to control us—because of what we believe they will give us. And the true test of idolatry is our response to its loss. Keller makes a key distinction between sorrow and despair: "Sorrow comes from losing one good thing among others. . . . Despair, however, is inconsolable, because it comes from losing an *ultimate* thing. When you lose the ultimate source of your meaning or hope, there are no alternative sources to turn to. It breaks your spirit."[4]

---

3. Timothy Keller, *Counterfeit Gods: The Empty Promises of Money, Sex, and Power, and the Only Hope That Matters* (New York: Dutton, 2009), xvii–xviii.
4. Keller, *Counterfeit Gods*, x–xi

As you think about loss in your life, or as you consider a season when tears and sadness were a daily experience, what did you learn about yourself? What lessons did you discover as you stood over the rubble of life? What idols did it surface?

Perhaps you are in a season of sorrow right now. Maybe your beaker has been bumped. I want you to know that there are important lessons to learn. I want to encourage you to allow your grief to show you what is surfacing in your heart. Let God uncover—layer by layer—the things in which you perhaps placed too much trust. In the same way that pain can be a platform for worship, it can also be a conduit for spiritual growth and repentance.

In the fourth chapter of Lamentations we find a helpful but uncomfortable lament. Soong-Chan Rah, in his book *Prophetic Lament*, suggests that this chapter highlights the way "symbols of success and power are deconstructed."[5] In other words, it mourns the idols upon which we place too much hope. In this way, lament not only expresses sorrow over a loss; it also mourns misplaced trust. When your culture or city or life falls apart, it can be revealing.

Let's unearth five potential expressions of idolatry that we find in Lamentations 4.

Fixating on Financial Security

Lamentations 4 begins by lamenting the loss of the security and glory of Jerusalem's wealth:

> How the gold has grown dim,
>   how the pure gold is changed! (v. 1)

The city of Jerusalem was the economic and spiritual center of Israel. The temple rose over the horizon with its grand

---

5. Soong-Chan Rah, *Prophetic Lament: A Call for Justice in Troubled Times* (Downers Grove: InterVarsity Press, 2015), 171.

architecture and gleaming jewels. The ark of the covenant, the walls of the sanctuary, the vessels and utensils, and even the shields were made from precious metals (1 Kings 6:20–22). Gold was everywhere.

This wealth made a statement, because gold is connected to glory. But now the gold is dim, and

> the holy stones are scattered
> > at the head of every street. (Lam. 4:1)

The city has lost its luster. The temple has been destroyed. Cherished symbols lie in a dust-covered heap of ruins. Any trust in what the temple and its gold represented has vanished.

I trust you know that money has power. It provides security. It creates identity. It gives options. If we are not careful, money can fuel self-sufficiency. That's why a recession, the loss of a job, the failure of a business, or a city with shuttered factories is an opportunity to reflect on our misplaced trust in our paper-thin financial security. When a 401(k) loses its value, or a downsizing announcement arrives in your inbox, lamenting the loss can awaken your soul to the foolishness of trusting in financial security.

The security of money or the fear of financial loss can easily become a functional god in our lives. Hardship or financial stress can reveal an idolatrous fixation with the security that money provides.

A few years ago my wife and I were trying to purchase a foreclosed home in order for my mother-in-law to move in with us. The home was going to require a total interior renovation. For it to work, we had to sell our existing home, find transitional housing, and figure out how to manage such a huge construction project. I spent hours developing spreadsheets, reviewing costs, talking to contractors, and running financial models. At one level I wanted to make a good decision. But even more, I feared making a big mistake.

However, my research subtly shifted from good stewardship to self-centered anxiety. The numbers and options started to consume every spare moment of my thinking. Worried I was missing something, I kept checking and rechecking my numbers. I started losing sleep. My prayer times were scattered.

It took the lament of a funeral to wake me up.

Friends of our family were walking through the death of their teenage son. It was tragic. He had taken his life. Sitting in the back of the church, I listened to our friends talk about their grief and joined in the sorrow that filled the room. During the funeral, my heart was convicted about my anxiety over my house project. What was I worrying about? Why was I allowing the project to consume me? The contrast between the concerns of our friends and mine was deeply convicting. An idol was exposed as I entered into our friends' lament.

I walked into the funeral fixated on financial security. My "burden" seemed heavy. But the service gave me much-needed perspective. My worries and fears about money seemed shallow and foolish in light of what I was witnessing in the funeral. As I sat in the back, I prayed, repented, and asked the Lord to forgive me—yet again—for my self-sufficiency.

Money can be a common idol beneath the surface of our lives. Do you know its subtle captivity? For you it could be the image of success, the temporary satisfaction of something new, the assurance of providing for your family, or the security of your future. Regardless of the expression, it is easy for money to become an object of trust. When loss or uncertainty enter the equation, it's remarkable how quickly this idol rears its ugly head. Lament penetrates the vault of our self-sufficiency and shows us the spiritual bankruptcy of trusting in financial security.

Treating People like Saviors

Suffering can also reveal a second object of misplaced trust: people. We can come face-to-face with how much we believe people can fix the problems around us. Whether it's politics, business, or religion, we can easily pin our hopes on others. That is part of the reason we are so enamored with fame and power. We live vicariously through those who lead us. We believe life will be better if "our people" are in control.

Lying in the rubble of Jerusalem was not only the gold but also any hope that a leader could fix the mess of the people's lives. The culture of the nation was broken like "earthen pots" (Lam. 4:2), and there was no one to stop the destruction. The wealthy were rummaging through the ash heaps (Lam. 4:5). Princes, known for beauty and fame, were now deformed and unrecognizable (Lam. 4:8–9). Even the king was captured. Jeremiah 39:1–10 records the tragic events surrounding King Zedekiah's arrest as he fled the city. His children were slaughtered, his eyes were gouged out, and he was deported to Babylon. Lamentations 4:20 helps us to feel the symbolic value of this disheartening moment:

> The breath of our nostrils, the LORD's anointed,
>   was captured in their pits,
> of whom we said, "Under his shadow
>   we shall live among the nations."

This lament reminds us that there are limitations to human leadership. The power of man-made government, the theories of economics, and the security of national defense are not ultimate. These systems and those who lead through them are frail.

Lament reminds us about the danger of putting too much hope in human leaders. The book of Lamentations warns us that our deliverer does not occupy a seat on the Supreme Court, reside at 1600 Pennsylvania Avenue, sit in the boardroom of a company, or stand behind a pulpit in our church. Seasons of uncertainty and loss reveal the vanity of putting our ultimate hope in anyone but God.

This is true at a personal level as well, including our closest relationships. Although a good friend can be helpful when you are walking through pain, he or she will never be able to bring complete healing to your heart. There's a gap in your soul that no mere human can fill. Try to have a friend play that role, and disappointment is sure to follow. Try to occupy that space in someone else's heart, and you'll be frustrated. Treating other people or ourselves like saviors is a subtle form of idolatry because our trust should rest in God alone.

This was a hard lesson for me to learn. As Sarah and I walked through the death of Sylvia and our season of lament, I realized there was a part of Sarah's heart I was not able to reach. My encouragement, prayers, and hugs, while helpful, were not sufficient to stop the pain. I could walk with her, but I couldn't heal her. I simply couldn't halt the grief in my wife's heart. As hard as I tried, sorrow remained.

Thankfully, Sarah never placed that expectation on me. I was the one trying to fill that space. Over time God brought the healing we both needed. But I often lamented my inability to completely help her. My laments not only expressed my sorrow but also helped me see how I can become my own idol.

Is a loss in your life revealing an excessive trust you place in others? Is it possible you are trying to fill the gap of grief with their affection or attention? It can look like putting unrealistic expectations on a friend, a pastor, a spouse, or your children. What's more, grief can turn you inward, as you attempt to overanalyze your way forward. Remember, the first step in lament is turning to God—not to your closest relationships, and certainly not to yourself.

Lamentations 4 helps us to see the vanity of making any-one—including ourselves—the ultimate objects of trust.

Craving Cultural Comfort

The dark clouds of desperation over Jerusalem changed the way people treated one another. And it wasn't for the better. There was an erosion of social values. The people were cruel, neglecting even compassion that animals give their offspring (Lam. 4:3). Helpless nursing children were starving. When they begged for food, "no one [gave it] to them" (Lam. 4:4). Hope-lessness settled in the city, and the people wished for death (Lam. 4:9).

The point of this dark material is to show the complete unraveling of the social fabric in Jerusalem. Cultural norms collapsed as the city and nation crumbled. Basic relationships were dysfunctional. Compassion was gone.

Jeremiah uses lament to shine a bright light on this degra-dation. He mourns the loss as a warning of how broken our society can become.

As our church walked through Lamentations, we wanted lament to shine a bright light on the social ills of our culture as well. We did this because it is easy to ignore the brokenness and cruelty around us. The northern suburbs of Indianapolis are great places to live. In fact, a national magazine recently ranked one community as the number one place to live in America. The combination of safety, education, affordable homes, and high household incomes makes it the Disney World of suburbia.

However, peace and safety can create a heartless disregard for the problems under the surface or just a few miles away. It can be easy to insulate ourselves from cultural problems by retreating to the manicured lawns and gated communities of the suburbs. For example, less than five miles from our church is one of the largest abortion clinics in Indiana. Hidden behind large pine trees along a busy road linking the suburbs with the city stands a nondescript building where unborn children are murdered every day. In one of my sermons on lament, I rehearsed the harrowing statistics that are easy to ignore: every day nearly 2,500 babies are aborted in the United States, and since *Roe v. Wade*, over 60 million babies have lost their lives. And then I called upon our church to mourn:

> So let us lament the millions of children who were never born. Let us lament the shedding of innocent blood in our land. Let us lament the moment when a mother decides that her body is more valuable than a baby's body. Let us lament the trafficking of convenience, expediency, and even the body parts of aborted children. Let us lament the "spin" language that makes abortion pro-choice. Let us lament the pain and regret that some have to battle every day. Let us lament a culture for which this issue has become far too common and much too tolerable.

A few Sundays later I invited a lawyer in our church who serves on the Indiana Coalition to End Sexual Assault to lead us in another lament. He works with high-profile leaders, including professional athletes, to raise awareness and coordinate efforts with law enforcement. He shared a heart-wrenching summary of the problem of sexual assault in our community:

> Shockingly, Indiana ranks as the second worst state in the country for instances of sexual assault of high school–aged girls. We have a growing problem of child sexual abuse all over our state, often that goes unreported for years. Sex-trafficking, a problem we often think about on the other side of the world, is happening right here in Indiana. And the average age of a victim is twelve to fourteen years old.

There was a sober stillness in the sanctuary. People felt the weight of his words. Few knew that Indianapolis was a crossroads for the exploitation of young women. Before we were led in a lament prayer, he exhorted the congregation: "These atrocities must move us to lament. Let these words sink in. Be moved to lament; be moved to pray. And be moved to act—to make a difference."[6] Prayers of lament can give us new eyes to see the true condition of our society. Rather than holding the groan of our culture at a distance or ignoring it altogether, lament has the potential to open our hearts to enter into the pain. It can topple the idol of wanting to live in Mayberry, an idealistic world insulated from the problems around us.

What are the cultural issues you tend to ignore? Perhaps you can take a few minutes in your next prayer time to join the groans of your neighbors or your city. Talk to God about the challenges of generational poverty, divorce, teen pregnancy, racism, unemployment, drug addiction, and any other social ill you can remember. As you read or watch the news, let it move you to lament rather than despair or disgust. Allow lament to soften your heart to the problems around you.

Lament calls us not to ignore the cries of our culture.

Idolizing Spiritual Leaders

A cultural crisis directly affects relationships with spiritual leaders. In Lamentations, moral authority vanished, and the text mourns the loss of credibility among those who were supposed to be righteous. The spiritual leaders were complicit in the decay of the nation (Lam. 4:13), and they reaped the tragic consequences. Jeremiah describes these leaders as wandering, blind, isolated, and defiled (Lam. 4:14). The people call them "unclean!" (Lam. 4:15), an ironic charge, given the position of

---

6. Used by permission.

purity spiritual leaders were to maintain. Their honor vanished (Lam. 4:16). In short, the religious leaders lost their credibility and influence. They became fugitives in their own broken culture.

Lamentations 4 shows us how far spiritual leaders can fall. A lament like this should be a somber warning for those in spiritual leadership. Spiritual apathy from religious leaders was one reason why Israel lost its way. The lament of chapter 4 shows us the connection between a vacuum of spiritual leadership and divine discipline.

Rather than trying to leverage the church's political capital to win the culture wars, we ought to take a close look in the mirror. Spiritual leaders should walk alongside their people and model self-examination and repentance. Exile provides an opportunity for God's people to lament spiritual drift, not only of a culture but also of the church. We could echo the lament of Daniel who prayed:

> O Lord, the great and awesome God, who keeps covenant and steadfast love with those who love him and keep his commandments, we have sinned and done wrong and acted wickedly and rebelled, turning aside from your commandments and rules. We have not listened to your servants the prophets, who spoke in your name to our kings, our princes, and our fathers, and to all the people of the land. To you, O Lord, belongs righteousness, but to us open shame, as at this day, to the men of Judah, to the inhabitants of Jerusalem, and to all Israel, those who are near and those who are far away, in all the lands to which you have driven them, because of the treachery that they have committed against you. To us, O LORD, belongs open shame, to our kings, to our princes, and to our fathers, because we have sinned against you. (Dan. 9:4–8)

The lost ground of spiritual authority might be regained if we were more careful to not idolize those in spiritual leadership and if spiritual leaders led in lament.

I witnessed my first church-discipline meeting in high school. I can still remember where I was sitting in the small sanctuary as the church family was asked to remain seated at the conclusion of a service. Our senior pastor stood before the church with a look of sorrow I had not witnessed before. His face was ash white.

With a heavy heart he shared that our gathering was the last step on a long road of disappointment. The Sunday school superintendent, a man I knew personally, had left his wife and children for another woman. From the outside, he appeared to be a model of Christlikeness and faithful service. But after multiple confrontations and appeals, he was unrepentant. There was a heavy sobriety in the room as the members voted to remove him from our church. We hoped that restoration would be in his future. The prayers of our leaders, the tears in the room, the call for self-examination, and the realization that leaders can fall were seared into my soul.

Leadership failure at any level is sobering. Lamentations 4 mourns the loss of spiritual authority, and it reminds us about the danger of resting upon the perceived spirituality of religious leaders. This lament invites us to recommit to faithfulness.

Presuming Divine Favor

The final potential idol relates to the assumption of the blessing of God. No nation would have greater reason to claim a most-favored status than Israel. They were God's chosen people. The Old Testament affirmed this. But divine favor does not give people permission to proudly ignore God's warnings. "Prior to Jerusalem's fall," says Soong-Chan Rah, "the Israelites had come to see themselves as a special people who had deserved and earned their great city, rather than recognize that everything they had accomplished was by the grace of God."[7]

Lamentations makes it clear that the nation was under the discipline of the Lord. Jeremiah uses shocking language. He describes their chastisement as greater than Sodom (Lam. 4:6). In verse 11, we read, "The LORD gave full vent to his wrath." There was a foreboding sense that their days were numbered and that the end was drawing near (Lam. 4:18). The blessing of God was covered with a cloud.

The culture of the United States is enamored with optimism. The "American Spirit" is the deeply rooted belief that life will get better, recessions will end, opportunities will abound, and "the sun will come up tomorrow." While I appreciate this optimism at one level, I wonder how many American Christians make cultural optimism an idol. Or how many directly connect this optimism to the belief that we are "blessed by God." Perhaps this is partly why some Christians react negatively to the effects of our exile status. It seems that we are unfamiliar with spiritual survival in a culture where a recession doesn't end and where the social structures continue to work against a bright future.

I fear that too many of us, including myself, are so emotionally and spiritually tied to this optimism that we don't know how to live in a culture reaping what it has sown. Throughout the centuries, Christians have found a way forward while their culture was hostile or falling apart.

By reading books like Lamentations, we are reminded that divine blessing does not guarantee a pain-free life or a receptive culture. Lament helps us to see the way believers persevered while living in a society rampant with idols. But it also allows us

---

to search our own hearts for the ways those idols have invaded our lives as well.

Lament is the song you sing when divine blessing seems far away. Lamentations 4 helps us see the subtle idols that lie under the surface. Financial security, people, cultural comfort, spiritual leaders, or divine favor are just a few of the mini-gods that can capture our hearts. Losing them, in part or whole, presents an opportunity to be reminded where our affections should lie. Lamenting the toppling of our cultural idols can reorient Christian exiles as to what King and what kingdom we were supposed to long for.

Not without Hope

I realize this is a heavy chapter. I've tried to be faithful to the tone and content of this chapter in Lamentations. But you need to know it is not without hope. In verse 22, Jeremiah promises that God will not prolong his people's exile longer than necessary. There is purpose behind the dark clouds.

The unearthing of idols is part of God's plan.

When pain topples our idols, lament invites self-examination. We can see more clearly the misplaced objects of trust that surface when the layers are peeled back. Pain helps us to see who we are and what we love.

As you walk through various moments of loss, don't miss the life-changing lessons that are part of the process. Emotional healing, while a good and right goal, should not be your only focus. This valley can be one of the most important learning opportunities of your life. Pain is an uncomfortable but helpful teacher. Rather than resisting the exposure of your misplaced trust, embrace the journey. Talk to God about what you are learning. Seek his forgiveness. Ask him to help you change.

Lamentations was written as a memorial for these lessons.

Over the last five years I've been encouraged by the shift taking place in my church and in subsets of Christian culture at large. Talking about being an exile is no longer uncommon. Rather than running to anger or fear, I'm hearing more lament. That's really good. What's more, I'm seeing people address the entanglement of their hearts with their culture.

Certainly we've not arrived. But in the process of wrestling with our exile, we are rediscovering the grace of lament. This ancient expression not only gives voice to our pain; it also becomes our teacher.

Lament shows us how to think and what to pray when our idols become clear.

Reflection Questions

1. How have you responded to the changes in our culture over the last ten years? What about your friends, your family, or people in your church?
2. Based on this chapter, what role could lament play in navigating these changes in the culture?
3. How can loss or suffering reveal our idols—the things on which we place our trust? When have you seen this in your own life?
4. As you read through the types of idols, which does your heart tend to gravitate toward? Why do you think they are so attractive to you?
5. How can lament serve us when the culture doesn't seem to be in crisis or is stabilized? How might the biblical song of sorrow in Lamentations 4 serve as a wake-up call?
6. What other idols do you need to lament over? What areas of cultural upheaval do you need to mourn?

8

A Road Map to Grace

Lamentations 5

Restore us to yourself, O LORD.
Lamentations 5:21

There are no "and they lived happily ever after" moments in Lamentations.

This historic lament concludes without resolution and with questions lingering. It ends by telling us where to look in pain, not by giving us the rest of the story. We'd need to look elsewhere in the Bible for what transpired after the destruction of Jerusalem. However, this lament is still filled with hope because of where it points us.

So far in part 2, we've learned from lament by observing the reality of a broken world and a holy God, the hope that comes from truth rehearsed, and the way loss can reveal our idols. This final chapter helps us see lament as the language of spiritual reorientation. Lament identifies the way back to God and even the gospel itself.

Lament can be a road map to God's grace.

A man named Brian is an attorney with the Neighborhood Christian Legal Clinic. Every day he uses his legal skills to relieve injustice in Indianapolis. He advocates for people whose poverty makes them targets for abuse. He sees community pain daily. But Brian and his wife, Melissa, had a front-row seat to a new tragedy a few years ago. In a moment of personal crisis, they learned the value of lament. Actually, they learned how to lead in lament.

Brian and Melissa lived in a quiet neighborhood on the West Side of Indianapolis, a middle-class community of young families, playgroups for kids, and caring neighbors. The kind of neighborhood filled with children laughing on play sets, bikes everywhere, and backyard barbecues. But on November 10, 2015, their peaceful neighborhood was shattered by a home invasion and a brutal murder.

One morning three armed men targeted a neighbor's home. It belonged to a young couple who moved to Indianapolis with a dream of planting a church. After the husband left for the gym, the men entered the home. Amanda, a pregnant twenty-eight-year-old mother, was murdered while their toddler slept in his crib. The senseless slaying shook the city and drew the attention of national media.

The police interviewed neighbors, reviewed security footage, and searched the city for the three men. Meanwhile Brian and Melissa, along with another couple from our church, walked their neighbors through the grief that invaded their neighborhood. They opened their home for lament. The first night over fifty neighbors crowded their living room to read the Bible, pray, and weep together. Many were believers; others were not. But all of them were in pain. The tragedy brought them together. Brian became their guide.

Every weekday evening for three weeks, Brian and Melissa's home became a place of lament. As they waited for the suspects to be caught and as their neighbors tried to recover, they used Psalm 13 as their base text. They cried out together, "How long, O LORD!" allowing it to direct them toward trust and worship. Over the weeks, the size of the group varied, but Brian's home became a sanctuary for sorrow.

As the believers in Brian's neighborhood entered the pain and fearful questions of their neighbors, the believers were able to give their neighbors a path toward hope. Lament opened the door for many important spiritual conversations.

Lamentations 5: A Road Map to God's Grace

The final chapter of Lamentations ends without resolving the destruction of Jerusalem, but it points readers in the right direction. Suffering lingers. The temple still lies in ruin. There is more to come, but the answer has not arrived. Yet the book ends with a hopeful prayer:

> Restore us to yourself, O LORD, that we may be restored!
>   Renew our days as of old—
> unless you have utterly rejected us,
>   and you remain exceedingly angry with us.
>   (Lam. 5:21–22)

The final chapter of Lamentations is unique. While it continues to highlight themes regarding the devastation of Jerusalem, it doesn't follow the poetic pattern of the other chapters. The verses are much shorter, almost staccato-like in their wording—a rapid-fire summary of grief. And while you could find every element of lament in this chapter (turning, complaining, asking, trusting), there is a particular focus on requests made directly to God. Chapter 5 looks to God for hope.

You may have picked up this book hoping that lament would untie all the knots of pain in your life. But answers to prayer and resolution of painful questions do not usually come quickly. Sometimes the answer is not what we'd want or request. The timing may be much slower than we'd hoped. Lament is the prayer language for these gaps. It tells you where to look and whom to trust when pain and uncertainty hang in the air you breathe. When brokenness becomes your life, lament helps you turn to God. It lifts your head and turns your tear-filled eyes toward the only hope you have: God's grace. I hope you are encouraged by this.

Do you remember where we started our journey in learning to lament? In chapter 1, I encouraged you to keep turning to God in prayer. I cautioned you about deafening silence—prayerlessness. The first step in lament pushes against this by calling us to keep praying. And as Jeremiah's lament ends, we hear the same invitation. We must keep praying.

We must keep lamenting. And we must help others to do the same.

Lamentations concludes with three prayers that serve as directional markers for the journey ahead. These prayers serve as a guide, showing us what to pray when the future is not clear. I hope they'll become your road map to God's grace.

"Remember, O Lord . . ."

Chapter 5 begins with an appeal for God to remember:

> Remember, O Lord, what has befallen us;
>   look, and see our disgrace! (Lam. 5:1)

This request is more than asking God not to forget. For God to remember captures the essence of his grace to his people as their covenant keeper. "Remember" is a request for God to intervene based on his love and promises. It is a call for God to act. The Bible frequently connects God's redemption to this gracious remembering. A few examples:

- After the judgment of the flood, Genesis 8:1 says that "God remembered Noah."
- In Genesis 9, God promises to never destroy mankind in a flood again: "I will remember my covenant that is between me and you. . . . When the bow is in the clouds, I will see it and remember the everlasting covenant" (Gen. 9:15–16).
- When the Israelites sinned with the golden calf, Moses pleaded with the Lord to be merciful by remembering his covenant with Abraham, Isaac, and Jacob (Deut. 9:27).
- And David cried out to the Lord for mercy in Psalm 25 on the basis of God's "remembering": "Remember your mercy, O Lord, and your steadfast love, / for they have been from of old. / Remember not the sins of my youth or my transgressions; / according to your steadfast love remember me, / for the sake of your goodness, O Lord!" (Ps. 25:6–7).

I could give you other examples, but the point should be clear enough. When Jeremiah asks God to remember, he appeals for grace based on God's character. He's seeking assurance that this destruction is not pointless. Jeremiah is asking God for help.

Central to this appeal is the feeling of shame. That's why he says, "See our disgrace" (Lam. 5:1). Have you ever tried to hide your tears? Crying is embarrassing. Hardship is humbling. In Israel's case, suffering devastated their temple, humiliated their leaders, destroyed their city, and ruined their nation. But instead of running from the shame of sorrow, lament embraces it. Lament looks through the fog for the grace of God's remembrance.

The road map to grace involves an appeal for God to remember while at the same time rehearsing the pain. This is similar to what we learned through the lament psalms— a heartfelt cry of complaint. Verses 2–18 (the bulk of Lamentations 5), paint a dismal picture: Foreign invaders have destroyed the nation (v. 2). The people feel abandoned (v. 3), survival is very hard (v. 4), and they are exhausted (v. 5). They must appeal to foreign nations (v. 6) while bearing the consequences of national sins (v. 7). Upheaval marks their culture (v. 8) while desperation and hunger are everywhere (vv. 9–10). Women are violated (v. 11), princes are dishonored (v. 12), and oppression rules the day (v. 13). Celebrations have ceased (vv. 14–15). The glory of Israel has vanished (v. 16), and hopelessness has set in (v. 17). Wild animals now roam the streets (v. 18). Of the twenty-two verses in chapter 5, seventeen of them carry this tone.

But this rehearsing of pain has a purpose.

The full-throttle cataloging of pain sets the context for the call for God to remember. However, it has been my experience that many Christians are uncomfortable with the tension of the long rehearsing of pain combined with the appeal to God's grace. We tend to hush the recitation of sorrow. However, restoration doesn't come to those who live in denial. I wonder what would happen if more Christians confidently walked into the darkest moments of life and guided people in talking to God about their pain.

Maybe that's why an article titled "Why Charlotte Exploded and Tulsa Prayed" caught my eye. It was written after two black men, Terence Crutcher and Keith Lamont Scott, were shot and killed by police officers in Tulsa, Oklahoma, and Charlotte, North Carolina. These incidents were part of a series of officer-involved shootings of black men that resulted in protests around the country.

This article vividly portrayed two different responses. It featured images of Charlotte with violent clashes between police and protestors. In contrast, it highlighted people praying inside a church in Tulsa. According to the reporter, the critical difference was Rev. Ray Owens at Metropolitan Baptist Church in Tulsa. As racial conflict boiled to the surface, he opened his church for a prayer vigil. But the prayer meeting was not merely a vigil for Terence Crutcher, nor was it only a place to pray for unity.

It was a place to lament—a place to call upon God to remember.

As tension filled the city of Tulsa and rumors of protests spread, people began asking Pastor Owens where they could go to cry and share how they felt. He wisely hosted a lament service. Among other prayer forms, Pastor Owens distributed index cards. He invited people to write out their painful feelings and frustrations and to post them in the church. His aim was to make the church a place for "safe yet constructive expression of our righteous rage."[1] One card said, "We want justice and peace!"[2] Pastor Owens served the city of Tulsa not only as a comforter but also as a leader in lament.

One of my hopes from this book is for more believers and churches to step into the space of people's pain and community sorrow with the liturgy of lament. I long to see this happen at

---

1. Amanda Wills, Sara Sidner, and Mallory Simon, "Why Charlotte Exploded and Tulsa Prayed," CNN, September 22, 2016, www.cnn.com/2016/09/22/us/tulsa-charlotte-shooting-protests/index.html.
2. Wills, Sidner, and Simon, "Why Charlotte Exploded."

a personal level but also with larger groups or communities. Chapter 10 explores this application in detail. My point is simply that those who know the story of God's "remembering" should lead the way in talking to God about pain or outrage. There is a road map for walking through the pain of loss, and it starts by asking God to remember our struggle. But that is not the only prayer in Lamentations 5.

"But You, O Lord, Reign Forever"

We learned in the Psalms about the importance of words like *but* and *yet*. After the long record of the devastation in the first eighteen verses of Lamentations 5, Jeremiah says, "But you, O Lord, reign forever" (Lam. 5:19). In this closing chapter of Lamentations we find another example of spiritual reorientation. Jeremiah reconnects his heart to what he believes: God is sovereign over everything, including our pain.

Jeremiah affirms the rule of God. He confesses that everything works according to the decree and purpose of the Creator. God is in control. Every event in life moves toward the fulfillment of the plan he ordained. He reigns forever.

The reign of God was a major theme in Jeremiah's life and prophetic ministry. God called Jeremiah to be a prophet before he was born (Jer. 1:5). The nation was compared to a pot in the hands of a potter: "Behold, like the clay in the potter's hand, so are you in my hand, O house of Israel" (Jer. 18:6). And in one of the most telling passages, God affirms his power to do anything—even giving Jerusalem over to the Babylonians. "Behold, I am the Lord, the God of all flesh. Is anything too hard for me? Therefore, thus says the Lord: Behold, I am giving this city into the hands of the Chaldeans and into the hand of Nebuchadnezzar king of Babylon, and he shall capture it" (Jer. 32:27–28).

Don't forget that in Lamentations 5:2–18 Jeremiah has just recounted a long list of troubles. But now he says, "But you . . . reign forever."

You might wonder how this is comforting or helpful. Life often feels like it is out of control. God may feel distant. Evil appears to be winning the day. I'm sure you've felt that way many times. I certainly have. Or maybe you are walking with someone whose storyline appears to be cruel. Lamentations shows us that God's sovereignty and his reign are not negated by suffering. God is still in control, even through loss.

Lament affirms God's sovereignty when dark clouds linger.

I don't know how many times I've laid my head on the pillow and said, "Lord, I'm trusting you're in control tonight." Every day is filled with great gaps of uncertainty. Pain makes that gulf wider and more overwhelming. But books like Lamentations help us trust the God who wrote the rest of the story beyond chapter 5. He reigns when the future is unclear.

One of my favorite passages to read when I'm struggling to trust in God's sovereignty is in the second chapter of Acts. It is part of Peter's sermon after Pentecost. He says: "This Jesus, delivered up according to the definite plan and foreknowledge of God, you crucified and killed by the hands of lawless men. God raised him up, loosing the pangs of death, because it was not possible for him to be held by it" (Acts 2:23–24). God ordained (reigned over) Jesus's crucifixion. The cruel death of the Son of God at the hands of wicked men was part of God's plan. And here's the thing: if God can take the most unjust moment in history and turn it into redemption, then surely we can say, "You reign!" Even when we can't imagine how God might use hard circumstances in our lives, we can still believe he's in control.

I wouldn't be writing this book without the death of Sylvia. Without an empty crib and a lifeless newborn, lament would be unknown to me. But God reigned through those times. And he's still reigning. I've seen it personally. And I'm sure you have as well. So, when we struggle under the weight of hard circumstances, we need to remind our hearts that God reigned through the cross. The Bible has told us the redemptive story so we can find our way through the darkest moments of life.

Let the book of Lamentations encourage you. Don't fear specifically identifying the pain in your life. But don't allow it to reign either. As you walk the shadowlands of pain, look for opportunities to remind your soul about God's sovereign control. Remember the words of William Cowper:

> Behind a frowning providence
>   He hides a smiling face.[3]

Prayerfully celebrate the reign of God even when you have no idea how the plan will unfold.

The presence of pain—no matter how strong—does not negate the plan of God. He still reigns. Therefore, we can tearfully pray one last prayer in Lamentations.

"Restore Us to Yourself, O Lord"

The longest lament in the Bible ends with a prayer for restoration. As we've seen through our journey, lament prayers cry out to God and ask him for deliverance: "God, this hurts! Please help me!" The book of Lamentations ends with the same focus and tone. It is the final mile-marker on the path of grace. In fact, the word "restore" is used twice, and we also hear the word "renew."

> Restore us to yourself, O Lord, that we may be restored!
>   Renew our days as of old. (Lam. 5:21)

---

3. H. Stebbing, *The Complete Poetical Works of William Cowper* (New York: D. Appleton, 1869), 405.

These words have specific meaning. The word "restore" could also be translated as "return" or "turn back."[4] Repentance and spiritual restoration are in mind here. Jeremiah's prophetic ministry was known for this kind of message. "Restore and return" were the central messages of his life.

Closely connected to the prayer for restoration is the longing for renewal. The request "renew our days as of old" seeks the kind of divine favor and blessing that was a part of Israel's history. However, the desire expressed is more than the rebuilding of the ruins of Jerusalem. It is a longing for a heart-based renewal. It's the prayer of David in Psalm 51:10:

> Create in me a clean heart, O God,
> and renew a right spirit within me.

Jeremiah pleaded with the people to return to the Lord, and the destruction of Jerusalem was part of God's plan to awaken the hearts of his people and bring them back to himself (Jer. 18:11). That's why the last verse of Lamentations includes the dark tone of God's judgment:

> . . . unless you have utterly rejected us,
> and you remain exceedingly angry with us. (5:22)

The sorrow behind Lamentations has its roots in divine discipline. The nation strayed from faithfulness, and God will use pain in order to renew them.

This final prayer for renewal is not only what they needed but also what God promised. It is another example of spiritual alignment through lament. This prayer agrees with God about what is ultimately needed and what God promised. It points the way toward God's grace.

---

4. Francis Brown, Samuel Rolles Driver, and Charles Augustus Briggs, *Enhanced Brown-Driver-Briggs Hebrew and English Lexicon* (Oxford: Clarendon, 1977), 996.

God promised that one day he would give his people new hearts. Theologians see this fulfilled in the new covenant. It addresses the brokenness that lies inside all our hearts:

> For this is the covenant that I will make with the house of Israel after those days, declares the LORD: I will put my law within them, and I will write it on their hearts. And I will be their God, and they shall be my people. . . . For I will forgive their iniquity, and I will remember their sin no more. (Jer. 31:33–34)

The prophet Ezekiel, a contemporary of Jeremiah, echoed the same hope. "And I will give you a new heart, and a new spirit I will put within you. And I will remove the heart of stone from your flesh and give you a heart of flesh. And I will put my Spirit within you, and cause you to walk in my statutes and be careful to obey my rules" (Ezek. 36:26–27). So the prayer for restoration and renewal at the end of Lamentations points to something that only God can do.

Lament can tune your heart to seek more than just the removal of pain. It invites us to say "remember, O LORD," "you reign," and "restore us." And in asking for God to deliver us, it can also lead us to the greatest need of all: our need to be right with God.

A Road Map to Christ

Lament is the language of a people who know the whole story—the gospel story. They know how the entrance of sin into the world brought death and suffering. As we conclude our look into Lamentations, it is a good reminder that the message of the gospel is where lament should lead. The sorrow of loss can lead us to the man of sorrows because Jesus is the answer to the cause of every pain.

Every sorrow, every tear, and every loss gives evidence of the brokenness caused by sin. Something is terribly wrong with our culture and inside of us.

Christians know that sin creates the pain behind lament.

However, under the dark clouds of brokenness, God offers mercy. The Son of God was sent on a mission: become a man, be perfectly obedient, and die on a cross to provide restoration. As Jesus hung between heaven and earth, he absorbed the wrath of God for those who would trust him. It was the darkest day in human history, and yet it changed everything.

After three days, the empty tomb testified to Jesus's victory. The resurrection of Christ signaled the coming defeat of the Devil and even of death itself. And with this victory, the Christian's view of pain and suffering in this present life is transformed: "For I consider that the sufferings of this present time are not worth comparing with the glory that is to be revealed to us" (Rom. 8:18). So we, along with all creation, groan as we wait for the future day when Christ's victory will be complete. We lament. We embrace this language of sorrow as a road map to God's grace.

Remember Brian, the man who led his neighbors in lament? Well, there's more to the story. Two months after the shooting and the subsequent arrest of the three men involved, Brian and Melissa opened their home again. The conversations about lament led to a four-week study of a book on suffering. Believers and nonbelievers attended, wrestling with God's purpose in their pain.

Brian helped his neighbors discover how the Bible speaks into the full range of human emotions, including doubt, fear, anger, and overwhelming sorrow. He explained the brokenness of the world as the cause of all pain and highlighted the biblical vision for restoration that comes through Jesus when he makes all things new. The tragedy in their neighborhood allowed Brian and the other believers not only to enter their neighbors' sorrow but also to point them to the ultimate hope in Jesus.

I hope you now understand how lament can be our teacher. The book of Lamentations shows us how a song of sorrow can remind us about the brokenness of the world, invite us to rehearse hope-filled truth, and confront our idols. Lament can also become a pathway to God's grace. Laments are memorials, vital records of lessons to be learned.

Christians can enter the rubble of life and even lead in lament because we know the rest of the story. We can open our hearts, our voices, and our homes to people who desperately want restoration but have no idea where to find it.

Dark clouds can yield deep mercy as lament leads to Christ.

Reflection Questions

1. Why do you think Christians are reluctant to step into the pain of other people's lives or into the pain of a community? What are the dynamics involved?
2. How can it be helpful to prayerfully rehearse our pain while asking God to "remember"?
3. What verses elsewhere in the Bible might give you confidence to take that step?
4. In your own words, how would you define the sovereignty of God? At what point in your life has this doctrine been a struggle? When has it been comforting?
5. Take some time to read Jeremiah 31:33–34 and Ezekiel 36:26–27 again. How do these passages shape your understanding of restoration?
6. How can lament lead to the gospel? What would lament sound like, or what words would you say in using the language of loss as a bridge to the cross?

7. Is there anything on the horizon of your life, in your sphere of relationships, or in your community that might be an opportunity for you to guide others through lament to the gospel?

8. Spend some time asking the Lord to open doors and to give you the courage to walk through them.

PART 3

———— ♦ ————

LIVING WITH LAMENT

PERSONAL AND COMMUNITY
APPLICATIONS

9

Making Lament Personal

Show me how you lament, and I will tell you who you are.
(author unknown)

Every lamenter has a story.

Pain in your life or in a loved one's life probably led you to this book. Perhaps you were seeking hope as you tried to pick up the pieces of your life. Maybe you wanted to understand the kind of prayers erupting from your heart as you wrestled with deep sadness. You might have been seeking to help a friend who seems inconsolable or in despair. Or you may be a ministry leader trying to learn how to help people process their pain.

Regardless of the circumstances that thrust you on this journey, I hope lament is becoming not only familiar but also life-giving. I hope you are seeing the potential of mercy under dark clouds. As we lay out our messy struggles, we can seek the help of a grace-giving God. In our sorrow, we can turn to prayer. We are able to vocalize the tension of our suffering and God's sovereignty. Lament rises from a firm belief in the character of

God, an understanding of the brokenness of sin, and a heartfelt longing for the completion of God's redemptive plan. That's why lament is inherently Christian.

Lament is a prayer in pain that leads to trust.

My personal and pastoral experience has shown me that lament can be a conduit of God's grace. I never intended to learn to lament. The Lord used the death of Sylvia to begin tuning my ear to this prayer language. Through the years, I unintentionally became a lover of lament because I began to see the ways it could be practiced and the unique help it offers. I don't know many people who intentionally study lament. It is not normally explored as an academic subject. And most people do not set out to learn *to* lament or to learn *from* lament.

Lament is usually a surprising personal discovery.

As I've said, my goal in this book is not merely to increase your understanding. I hope to encourage you to practice lament in more ways than you probably imagined when you first picked up this book. Growing in lament is connected to your personal spiritual growth and your view of God. As Esther Fleece says in her book *No More Faking Fine*, "Spiritual maturity does not mean living a lament-less life; rather, it means we grow into becoming good lamenters and thus grow in our need for God."[1]

In part 3 we are going to explore ways lament can be practiced from a personal or corporate perspective. We are going to move from learning *to* lament and learning *from* lament toward learning how to live *with* lament. Unexpected sorrow may have set you on this path, but there are many places yet to travel. I hope this biblical song of sorrow makes its way into many areas of your life or ministry. I want you to keep discovering

---

1. Esther Fleece, *No More Faking Fine: Ending the Pretending* (Grand Rapids, MI: Zondervan, 2017), loc. 37 of 219, Kindle.

ways lament can be applied so you can keep experiencing the mercy of God.

Wherever there are tears, there should be biblical lament.

Why Lament?

We've covered a lot of ground through our journey. As we explore some practical applications, let me remind you why lament should be your prayer when grief—of any kind—becomes a part of your life:

1. *It is a language for loss.* Lament is the historic prayer language for hurting Christians. It provides a biblical vocabulary and a model for talking to God about our pain or helping those who are walking through suffering.

2. *It is the solution for silence.* Too many Christians either are afraid or refuse to talk to God about their struggles. Whether because of shame, a fear of rejection, anxiety, or a concern of being irreverent, pain can give rise to a deadly prayerlessness. Lament cracks the door open to talk to God again—even if it's messy.

3. *It is a category for complaints.* Lament helps us see that complaining to God is not necessarily sinful. For hurting people, knowing that this expression of grief is a biblical and a God-given category can be a watershed moment. Vocalizing our pain or helping a friend express her heart is one of the life-giving aspects of lament.

4. *It is a framework for feelings.* This biblical song of sorrow is more than the sinful spewing of every emotion in your soul. Lament validates the expression of pain while providing a framework—a God-centered structure—so we avoid falling into the trap of self-centeredness, which can take root in times of deep sadness. Lament endorses expression, but only the kind with the right objective.

5. *It is a process for our pain.* Lament is more than a biblical version of the stages of grief (i.e., denial, anger, bargaining, depression, and acceptance). It invites God's people on a journey as they turn to God, lay out their complaints, ask for his help, and choose to trust. Embracing the ongoing—often daily—process of lament requires that we walk by faith. Lament is more than something that comes out of you. It is part of the process happening in you.

6. *It is a way to worship.* Too many people think real worship only means an upbeat and happy demeanor. But grief-filled prayers of pain while seeking God are among the deepest expressions of God-centered worship.

The Christian life should be marked by personal lament because, through this discovery, we open ourselves to God's grace and his ability to shape and change us. Since life is full of sorrows, opportunities abound to make lament a vital part of our spiritual journey. The key is to determine how.

In this chapter I'm going to suggest a number of steps you might take in personal lament or in helping others. I hope you'll find new applications to the discoveries you've already made. I want you to see the many ways lament can lead to God's grace.

Reading Scripture

This book is not the final word on lament. It barely scratches the surface of all that could be explored in this important topic. I hope our journey together inspires you to read the Bible with an eye for lament so you can keep learning how to apply lament in life-giving ways. Therefore, I want to encourage you not to limit your study to this book. We have examined only the book of Lamentations and four lament psalms. There are over forty more lament psalms, each one unique, occupying a special place in the sacred hymnal, and each could have an important role in your life. So keep reading and studying.[2]

While writing this book, I spent some extended devotional time in the lament psalms. I started to memorize Psalm 86. Additionally, I printed out one lament a day and marked up the text as I looked for the four elements (turning, complaining, asking, and trusting). The thematic framework became like 3-D glasses, allowing life lessons and applications to emerge out of passages I've read many times. Once you start reading the Bible this way, especially the Psalms, you'll find them speaking into loneliness, frustration, fear, mistreatment, and injustice. At the same time, they'll give encouragement, hope, and confidence. The variety and depth are stunning.

But don't stop there.

The Bible is packed with laments beyond the Psalms. They can be found in books like Job, Jeremiah, Ezekiel, and Daniel. As you read, you'll find lament in Ezra's confession in resettled Jerusalem (Ezra 9:6–15), Jonah's cry in the belly of the whale (Jonah 2), Hezekiah's reflective words after his brush with death (Isa. 38:10–20), and Habakkuk's struggle with God's purposes (Habakkuk 1).

In the New Testament you'll hear the apostle Paul lament his thorn in the flesh while trusting in God's grace (2 Cor. 12:7–10). You'll read Jesus's quotation of Psalm 22 while on the cross (Matt. 27:45–50). And you'll see the culmination of God's redemptive plan as the answer to the martyr's lament in Revelation 6:10: "O Sovereign Lord, holy and true, how long before you will judge and avenge our blood . . . ?"[3]

---

2. See appendix 2 for a list of lament psalms.
3. For a more comprehensive list see appendix A in Michael Card, *A Sacred Sorrow: Reaching Out to God in the Lost Language of Lament* (Colorado Springs: NavPress, 2005), 146–47.

By reading the Scriptures through the lens of lament, you'll begin to discover the variety of circumstances and personalities that are a vital part of this historical song of sorrow. This lament awakening will not only allow you to read the Bible more thoughtfully but also show you the wide-ranging expressions of sorrow-filled prayers that could be your own or the means of helping a hurting friend. You'll learn how this prayer language has served the people of God through the centuries, and how it could be the language for any season in your life or the life of someone close to you.

When you read the Bible, look for lament.

Grieving

Lament is the prayer language for those who are struggling with sadness. In particular, when our hearts become heavy, there is a desperate need for empathy. Nicolas Wolterstorff captures the heart of this when he writes: "What I need to hear from you is that you recognize how painful it is. I need to hear from you that you are with me in my desperation. To comfort me, you have to come close. Come sit beside me on my mourning bench."[4]

Lament for others' pain vocalizes understanding and compassion. That's why the psalms of lament are helpful. It's why a friend's grief-filled prayer for you is so meaningful. And it's also why your candid, messy prayer in pain can be refreshing. Lament brings comfort to the mourning bench by refusing to pretend "everything's fine" or to remain distant. Lament sits close.

Sometimes people think lament is only for gut-wrenching grief or life-altering tragedies. While many of us discover

---

4. Nicolas Wolterstorff, *Lament for a Son* (Grand Rapids, MI: Eerdmans, 1987), loc. 166 of 562, Kindle.

lament in crisis, it can also be applied in less intense situations. We can use the spiritual reorientation of turning, complaining, asking, and trusting for the "normal" griefs of life. When a friend misunderstands you, a child's behavior is embarrassing, your family finances are inadequate, or the flu has knocked you down, you can use lament to redirect your heart. When a conflict in your marriage is discouraging, the invitation to the wedding didn't come, your church's vitality is subpar, or your baby won't sleep through the night, let lament do its work in the ordinary grief of life.

Practicing lament in the more common frustrations and less severe sorrows not only brings comfort but also develops a fluency in the language of loss. The heart behind this book is to help you discover the grace of putting lament into practice in ways that fit with all the pains of life. Regardless of what is causing you sorrow, let me encourage you to keep lamenting. Keep turning to God in prayer. Keep complaining. Keep asking. Keep trusting. In the same way that working a muscle trains it to carry greater weight, the spiritual exercise in lament prepares us for future hardship.

Gary Witherall and his wife, Bonnie, were missionaries in war-torn Lebanon. After graduating from Moody Bible Institute, they felt the call to serve the physical and spiritual needs of Palestinian refugees at a medical clinic for pregnant women. The work was slow, tedious, and sometimes dangerous. But the Witheralls were committed. Through the struggles of missionary work, Gary's heart was tuned toward lament. The brokenness around him and the overwhelming spiritual needs created a sadness that he regularly took to the Lord in prayer. A broken heart created a well-worn path of lament. Little did he know how much he would need this conduit of grace.[5]

---

5. Gary Witherall in an interview with the author, December 1, 2017.

Tragically, in 2002 a gunman walked into the medical clinic where Bonnie served. He began shooting. Bonnie was targeted and shot three times in the head.

Gary received a frantic call from the medical clinic, and he was told to come quickly. When he walked into the clinic, he collapsed on the floor. In his book, *Total Abandon*, Gary describes his grief with great candor:

> Suddenly I was wrenched into a place I could never have imagined. . . . I was forced to fall and fall and fall into the abyss of grief. I was not ready for this. I was not given time to prepare for the loss of the one person who lit up my world. *Boom*, there I was, forced into a world of agony. . . . I did not know I could cry so hard.[6]

Just feet away from where his wife gave her life, he was thrust into a new journey of lament. But in his overwhelming sorrow, Gary chose to cry out to the Lord. "I had to live in faith that God was in control, that Bonnie was with Jesus in heaven. I chose to believe the Bible, to believe that God knew, and now I needed to trust him. . . . I felt I was being called to lay down everything for him in surrender."[7]

In the midst of a torrent of grief and fear, Gary allowed lament to turn his heart once again toward God's grace and mercy. He was broken, and yet he prayed. And not just for himself. His lament gave him the strength to pray for the man who had taken his wife's life. Sorrow and tragedy could not extinguish Christ-centered mercy. Lament helped him get there.

In the months that followed, Gary continued his practice of lament. As he picked up the pieces of his life, mourned the loss of Bonnie, and wrestled with his future, songs of sorrow be-

6. Gary Witherall, with Elizabeth Newenhuyse, *Total Abandon* (Carol Stream: Tyndale, 2005), 91–92.
7. Witherall, *Total Abandon*, 93.

came a critical part of his healing and his future ministry. Bonnie's martyrdom and this new depth of lament shaped him in profound ways. This is why Gary believes lament is one of the highest forms of worship.[8] He's lived it. And I think he's right.

Gary's story is dramatic. Your story may never be as tragic. However, each of us has the opportunity to turn to lament regardless of the source or the severity of the pain. We need to learn *to* lament and *from* lament so that we can live *with* lament.

Regardless of the pain, lament is always the God-given path through grief.

Counseling

During formal or informal counseling, lament can be uniquely helpful as a framework for people who need spiritual guidance. Lament provides a helpful structure for a hurting person to process pain and feelings. Unfortunately, I've seen many grieving people falter spiritually. Some struggled because they were given a book on grief that turned them inward, causing them to overanalyze the source of every pain or nuances of what they were feeling. I've also seen people justify sinful responses as the "anger" stage of grief.

On the other hand, I've also spent time with grieving people who were treated with a lack of compassion. Well-meaning counselors applied truth without grace. Sometimes feelings were completely disregarded. At other times hurting people were given simplistic answers, a poorly applied Bible passage, and one-dimensional counsel to "renew their mind."

Lament provides a place for both feelings and truth.

The counseling ministry of our church uses lament psalms as an exercise for studying the progression of grief in the Scripture.[9]

---

8. Witherall, interview December 1, 2017.

9. I'm grateful for the work of Dr. Andrew Rogers, who developed a series of lament-oriented homework assignments for counselees at our church. He has written a helpful

By examining a lament psalm, the counselee is able to see first-hand the journey from gut-level honesty to God-centered worship. This anchors the counselee in a biblical expression of grief that feels familiar. It validates his or her struggle, but it also gives biblical direction to his or her thinking.

As a part of the exercise, the counselee has the opportunity to create a personal lament using the framework observed in the psalm. Working through each movement of lament allows people to think about and express their grief in a way that is instructive and spiritually helpful. This becomes a directional map for biblical thinking through heartfelt sorrow. To help you or anyone you are counseling, I've included in appendix 3 a worksheet I created based on the categories in part 1 of this book. I've also provided two filled-in examples. Give it a try.

Lament creates a powerful pathway for emotional restoration and spiritual growth while expressing pain and exulting in God. In this way, lament can become a helpful part of the counseling process. Feelings are expressed, grace is embraced, and the heart is renewed.

Overcoming Bitterness

"I'm so angry at them! How do I deal with my bitterness?" The question came as I was spending time with a church member. He'd been offended, and he tried talking to the person who had caused him pain. The conversation had not gone well. There was no ownership on the other person's part, even though he was clearly wrong. Resolution was a long way off. Now the offended person was angry—even bitter.

"I need to introduce you to imprecatory psalms—the kind of lament that talks to God about injustice," I replied. I took

---

article entitled "Complaining God's Way: Helping People Give Voice to Their Suffering," https://biblicalcounseling.com/2017/06/complaining-gods-way-helping-people-give-voice-suffering/.

a few minutes to explain that there is prayer language in the Bible for this kind of moment. I encouraged him to read lament prayers and even to pray his own. I knew that doing so had the potential to settle him down and turn his heart away from bitterness.

The lament psalms can help us when we are struggling with bitterness by providing an opportunity to talk to God about our pain and pray for those who've hurt us. Too often I find books dealing with bitterness tip toward what Chris Brauns, in his book *Unpacking Forgiveness*, calls therapeutic forgiveness—when we unconditionally forgive people so that we can deal with our pain.[10] We don't have time to explore this topic in full, and I know that there are different nuances of forgiveness. However, I'd like to suggest that laments help us find the balance between an appropriate desire for justice and the command to be merciful while having a forgiving spirit. Psalms of lament talk to God about pain and injustice so that we can "love our enemies and pray for those who persecute [us]" (Matt. 5:44), as well as "bless those who curse" (Luke 6:28).

Without deeply acknowledging the injustice of abuse, mistreatment, or unfairness, asking someone to unconditionally forgive an unrepentant person seems more influenced by secular psychology than by Scripture. Christians are certainly called to have a spirit of forgiveness and a willingness to reconcile (Mark 11:25; Eph. 4:32). But forgiveness and reconciliation have conditions (Matt. 18:15–17; Luke 17:3; 1 John 1:9).

Lament enters this complicated terrain by giving us a way to express our pain, long for justice, and pray for mercy on those toward whom we're tempted to be bitter. Rather than running to therapeutic forgiveness, the lament psalms—even

---

10. Chris Brauns, *Unpacking Forgiveness: Biblical Answers for Complex Questions and Deep Wounds* (Wheaton, IL: Crossway, 2008).

imprecatory psalms—can be a vital part of the solution for people struggling with bitter hearts.

Confessing Our Sins

Practicing lament can facilitate personal confession and a greater sensitivity to sin. Too often we may think of lament prayers as solely springing from external circumstances or the hurtful actions of others. But, as we learned in chapter 5, part of the brokenness of the world is the brokenness of sin in each of us. Even after we receive Jesus, we need to express sorrow to God for our sin.

There will be times when we reap what we've sown (Gal. 6:7). When our sin has proven costly, we can turn to laments like Psalms 6, 32, 38, 51, 102, 130, and 143, which express deep regret. These penitential psalms help us know what to say to God about our sin while reaffirming hope for forgiveness and future restoration. Michael Card illustrates this through David's laments and his hope in God's forgiveness in 2 Samuel 12:

> The same stubborn refusal to let go of God that is expressed in his laments empowered David to stubbornly refuse to be destroyed by the grief of innocent death and the despair of knowing it was all a consequence of his sin. The painful realities of death and sin had somehow been "dealt with" during his time of lament.[11]

Lament gives us a language for godly sorrow and a reason to hope again.

There's a second way that lament as confession can be helpful. Lament reminds us that even the small expressions of our

---

11. Michael Card, *A Sacred Sorrow: Reaching Out to God in the Lost Language of Lament* (Colorado Springs: NavPress, 2005), 83.

wayward hearts—those regular and "respectable" sins—are serious. Rather than limiting the penitential psalms to major moral failure, we can use the weight of lament to lead us to sensitivity to sin we might be inclined to ignore or neglect.

For instance, by reading the confession of Daniel 9 or Ezra 9, you might shudder at the effects of sin and be moved to make your own confession. You could read Psalm 32 or 51 while considering what sins in your life require the same kind of cleansing. In this way lament can shine the light on what we need to confess. It can remind us how much we need God's grace.

The seriousness of sin as seen through lament helps the soul keep the right perspective. Our failures are frequent enough and our brokenness deep enough that penitential laments should be a regular part of our spiritual rhythms.

Battling Loneliness

While there are many other applications, I want to end this chapter by considering how lament can help you when it feels as if no one else is struggling. In other words, how do you lament alone?

This is a unique kind of grief.

A crowd can be a lonely place when your heart is heavy. As a pastor, I've watched grieving people struggle as Sunday mornings felt emotionally distant from where they were living. Whether in the standard question "How are you?" or quick greetings with expected smiles, or the positive orientation in our singing, church can be emotionally challenging for deeply hurting people. I've known grieving church members who've struggled with a critical spirit and others who simply stopped coming to church altogether.

A man in our church fought this internal battle for years as his father's Alzheimer's disease brought on a low-grade sadness he struggled to shake. As we talked about this burden, he described Sundays as a bit like lemon juice in a paper cut. It made him more aware of the grief below the surface. The years-long good-bye to a father he loved made the cheerful greetings feel fake and the joyful singing seem incomplete. It's not that he was against either. But the pain in his life created an internal song of sorrow, not merriment.

I know how he feels. You may too. Or the day may come when you'll experience what he describes. When you are living in the land for which a third of the Psalms were written, it's important for you to know how to lament alone. I want to encourage you to embrace the loneliness. Now, I don't mean a gritty, resigned posture. Rather, I mean for you to practice private lament such that you can give a lot of grace to the rest of the world that isn't living with your pain.

I've often encouraged grieving people to spend some intentional lament time with the Lord throughout the week, and especially on Sunday mornings. Before you gather with other believers who will not understand, it would be helpful to linger in solitary lament. When you're hurting, I'm not sure any service, greeting, or group is going to fill the canyon in your soul. If you walk into those moments with high expectations, it will only magnify your pain. I've been there.

So, private lament—all alone with God—has the potential to bring healing to your soul and strength to your heart as you walk a lonely road.

Keep Trusting

Every lamenter has a story. Lament is a means of grace, no matter what trial you face. This biblical song of sorrow can become a personal pathway for mercy when darkness has settled in. I hope you are finding out how true that is through this book.

Let me encourage you to keep leaning into lament so that you "keep trusting the One who keeps you trusting."

Micah and Sherri were members of our church long enough to hear that John Piper quotation many times. It lodged in their hearts. But they never anticipated how they would learn to make it their own. Nor did they know how a heartfelt lament would be a turning point in their lives.

Sherri was pregnant with their second child when she went into preterm labor. The doctors attempted to stall the delivery process to give their unborn son more time to develop. The pregnancy was only twenty-seven weeks along, which meant substantial—even life-threatening—risks. The doctors' efforts worked for a few days, but despite their best attempts, Asa was born. He weighed less than three pounds. He had a long road ahead.

After eight weeks in neonatal intensive care, Asa suddenly took a dramatic turn for the worse. His little body began convulsing violently for almost twenty minutes. The seizures led the doctors to believe that Asa's brain was hemorrhaging or he had contracted meningitis. Regardless, the prognosis was dire. An MRI was ordered to confirm the bleak outlook. Micah and Sherri would have to wait two to three days for the news. Meanwhile, Asa's seizures continued.

During their torturous wait, Micah and Sherri retreated to a local fast-food restaurant. In the middle of this busy place, they bared their hearts to one another about their fears and what the future might hold. They mourned the possibilities and their struggle with contentment. They desperately wanted Asa to recover, and they acknowledged their internal battle to trust the Lord.

However, lingering over their lunch, Micah and Sherri poured their hearts out to the Lord. They talked to God about their fear and disappointment. They shared their sorrow about the seizures. They asked God for healing. But they also affirmed that God could be trusted—no matter the outcome. Through their pain they renewed their desire to keep trusting the One who keeps them trusting. It was a spiritual turning point.

The medical road ahead was long, but Asa's seizures stopped. The doctors still don't know what caused them or why they ceased. There were weeks of medical ups and downs, but eventually Asa came home. More medical challenges lay ahead. Complications and various therapies were a continual part of Asa's new life. Micah and Sherri couldn't take him near any crowds for over a year, including church. It was a hard road.

To memorialize their lament journey, Micah and Sherri constructed a large wooden plaque etched with the "Keep trusting" quotation. They mounted it on their living room wall. Every day Asa plays in a room where the words "Keep Trusting the One Who Keeps You Trusting" are just above his head.

Pain and hardship come in unexpected and unwelcomed waves. Lament is the personal song that expresses our grief while embracing God's goodness.

Everyone has a story. Lament is never a song you set out to sing. But in the discovery of lament, everyone can find grace for the pains of life.

Reflection Questions

1. How has your understanding and appreciation of lament changed by reading this book?
2. What do you think is lost for Christians if they fail to read the Bible with an eye to lament?
3. How has lament helped you deal with your own grief, or how do you anticipate it helping in the future?
4. If you are struggling with a bitter heart, how might lament start you on a path toward love and a willingness to forgive?

5. What confession lament might be helpful for you to write out? How could you incorporate this into your small group, Bible study, or Sunday school class?

6. Have you experienced a time of sorrow when you felt incredibly alone? How do you think private lament could have helped you?

7. In what painful areas of your life is it a struggle to "keep trusting" the Lord? Take some time to walk through four movements of lament (turning, complaining, asking, trusting).

10

Let Us Lament

Even if a verse or a psalm is not my own prayer, it is nevertheless the prayer of another member of the community.
Dietrich Bonhoeffer

"Pastor, when are we going to pray about Ferguson?"

The question was posed to me after a Sunday service by an African American brother named Jermaine. He's a formidable man. He still looks like he could run a football downfield with the strength and speed that marked his career at Indiana University and the NFL. I once made the mistake of guarding Jermaine during a pickup basketball game at a men's retreat. It was a painful experience.

However, it was the disappointment in Jermaine's eyes that struck me when he asked about Ferguson. My brother was clearly hurting.

I felt terrible.

And I didn't have a good answer.

A few weeks earlier, protests erupted in Ferguson, Missouri, related to the shooting of Michael Brown by a police officer. The scenes were troubling. City streets looked like a war zone with heavily armed officers, military-grade vehicles, and violent conflicts between protestors and the police. Two or three Sundays passed. I said nothing publicly.

I didn't understand the full picture of what was happening in Ferguson. Nor did I comprehend the grief in the hearts of our minority church members.

My silence was deafening.

After apologizing to him for missing yet another racially sensitive moment, I immediately changed course. We began praying about Ferguson, lamenting the racial strife, the violence, and the history of injustice—real and perceived—that lay beneath the surface of our culture. Our prayers attempted to communicate we cared. It was a start.

But our lament was painfully late.

The Ferguson miss became an important lesson for me. I still wince when I think about it. The conversation with Jermaine helped me realize how easily we neglect moments to lament together. Racial tension is just one of many examples where the body of Christ could be helped by entering into corporate lament. In fact, I now believe lamenting together is the church's calling— a unique voice in the darkness. And a failure to realize this not only neglects ministry opportunities but also sends the wrong message.

In this final chapter I want to offer some practical suggestions for ways groups of Christians, churches, and entire communities might lament together. I'd like to widen your horizon as you consider where you might lament with others, or how you can incorporate lament into the experience of biblical community. Perhaps you can become a leader in recovering this valuable language of sorrow.

Let's consider a number of areas related to corporate lament.

Funerals

Gathering because of the loss of a loved one would seem to be one of the most obvious places for lament. Funerals provide a unique opportunity to walk with grieving family and friends through this biblical song of sorrow. But think of the last time you actually heard a lament at a funeral?

It's strangely absent.

My experience over the years leads me to believe our funeral services are slightly out of balance. I think our motivations are right. We want to follow Paul's instruction to "not grieve as others do who have no hope" (1 Thess. 4:13). However, in the name of providing comfort, our funeral services are often marked by a subtle avoidance of talking about pain. Maybe it's because we think people are already sad enough. Perhaps it's because we want the message of hope to be the dominant theme. Again, I'm sure our intentions are right. But it just seems like a missed opportunity.

Consider the last funeral you attended. What was the service called? Probably a celebration of life. What was the prelude like? What passages were read? Were any lament psalms used? Did the pastor acknowledge the pain or the questions in the room and talk about them? Did anyone explain the spiritual message of death? Did the testimonies express the pain of the loss, or was it merely a recounting of funny stories?

I'm not suggesting our funeral services should be devoid of joyful hope and encouragement. But I wonder what we can learn from biblical lament as we think about funerals. We would be wise to learn how trust and praise are best expressed after an honest rehearsing of the pain and the questions that trouble our hearts. Pastors could help frame the purpose of a funeral as more than just a celebration of life but also an important place to bring our sadness, our struggles, and our questions. Readings from the lament psalms might be a part of the order of service. Testimonies could not only express the good memories but also set them in context of how deeply the person will be missed and why. Additional care could be given to the selection of music so that the right overall tone is set in the service—one that balances hope with sorrow.

Death is the Christian's enemy (1 Cor. 15:26). It vividly displays the brokenness of the world. It surfaces critical questions. Lament can provide language to express the depth of sorrow while leading us to hope, praise, and trust.

A funeral, of all places, could be—should be—a place to lament together.

Congregational Prayer

Another place for the application of lament is congregational prayer. Church leaders might consider how lament could have a more prominent role in the prayer times connected to the various gatherings of the church.[1] Since lament is a foreign concept to many contemporary evangelicals, hearing it modeled for them would be especially helpful. This could be as simple as praying through a psalm of lament or offering a heartfelt prayer over a crisis in the culture.

We've experimented with this in a few ways at our church. In chapter 7 I mentioned our lament prayers concerning abortion and sex trafficking. However, we try to incorporate corporate lament into our congregational prayers by featuring specific requests for people who are walking through suffering. As we pray for church members by name, we weep with real people

---

1. For two excellent articles on why to incorporate lament into worship gatherings and what lament sounds like, see Neal Woollard, "Why We Added a Prayer of Lament to Our Sunday Gathering," 9Marks (website), June 20, 2018, https://www.9marks .org/article/why-we-added-a-prayer-of-lament-to-our-sunday-gathering/, and Woollard, "What Does a Prayer of Lament Sound Like?," 9Marks (website), June 25, 2018, https:// www.9marks.org/article/what-does-a-prayer-of-lament-sound-like/.

through the loss of a child or groan together when cancer comes back. Even though our church has thousands of people who attend, this personalized lament allows us to intercede in an intimate and instructive manner.

Additionally, our service design team attempts to find creative ways to rehearse the gospel, including the confession of our sins. In one service, we featured a lament over our sins by reading a prayer of confession from the Book of Common Prayer together. There's something powerful hearing a congregation say, "We acknowledge and bewail our manifold sins and weakness, which we, from time to time, most grievously have committed by thought, word and deed."[2] Nothing sets up singing or a message of hope like a time to express sorrow over our sins.

We also allow time during our monthly prayer meeting for those who are walking through a trial to acknowledge their need and invite others to pray over them. We've lamented broken marriages, sexual sin, wayward children, joblessness, terminal illnesses, and any number of painful situations. During a prayer gathering near the Christmas season, we prayed for widows and widowers. Our purpose was to enter their loneliness by having brothers and sisters in Christ pray over them. We used lament to help us all bear the pain of these lonely believers. By creating space to lament together, we invite hurting people to come out of the shadows so others can join them in their journey.

My hope is for a resurgence of unique prayer times in the life of the church. The body of Christ needs to lament together. The church has been given this biblical prayer language, and we need each other to do it well.

We need to weep with those who weep.

---

2. "The Order for the Administration of the Lord's Supper," in the Book of Common Prayer (1928), accessed January 27, 2018, http://justus.anglican.org/resources/bcp/1928/HC.htm.

Preaching and Teaching

I've been preaching the Bible for almost twenty-five years. I've lost track of how many sermons I've preached. As I consider which messages seemed to have long-lasting impact, it's interesting to me that messages on Job, Psalms, and Lamentations top the list.

Over the years I've had a front-row seat at the healing grace of sermons that have given people a voice in their pain. In fact, I now try to build lament-oriented themes into my sermon planning or even weekly applications. When I think about how to apply the text, I not only imagine unsaved people, married and single adults, teenagers, and other such types of hearers. I also try to appeal to those who are walking through pain and to help them see how a particular text might help them turn, complain, ask, and trust as they grieve. If you teach the Bible, lead a small group, or have responsibility for a class, consider what role the minor key should play in your teaching plan.

This also relates to teaching tone. Steven Smith has written a helpful book titled *Recapturing the Voice of God*.[3] He suggests that the tone of the sermon should fit the tone of the text. I heartily agree.[4] Here is where I think fellow expositional, text-driven preachers might be helped. In our careful examination and explanation of the text, we need to be sure there is "tone alignment." In other words, you shouldn't preach lament like you preach Luke. The tone of the sermon can help people know what lament sounds like. When you discover laments in the Scripture, be sure to carefully exegete the meaning of the text. But don't stop there. Help people feel the text. Bring your heart to the meaning and application of lament.

---

3. Steven W. Smith, *Recapturing the Voice of God: Shaping Sermons Like Scripture* (Nashville: B&H Academic, 2015).

4. See, for example, my short article "Is Your Preaching Tone Deaf?," 9Marks (blog), June 18, 2015, www.9marks.org/article/is-your-preaching-tone-deaf/.

Preach about lament. Teach through your own lamenting. Apply the text to lamenters. Let the tone of lament be the tone of your sermon. As you do, you'll help your people learn the God-given prayer language of loss together.

Singing and Songwriting

The fourth area where lament could benefit the people of God is the songs we sing. The music of our churches both reflects and shapes the hearts of our people. Unfortunately, lament is virtually absent in most of our singing. This is not a new problem. The trend is concerning.

Soong-Chan Rah, in his book *Prophetic Lament*, cites a study of hymnals and their use of lament. It revealed that lament makes up less than 20 percent of Presbyterian and Baptist hymnals.[5] When one looks at the contemporary songs reflected through the copyright licenses (CCLI), the tracking of songs most frequently sung by churches, the trend is even more concerning. I surveyed recent songs in 2016 and 2017. The number of lament-oriented songs was well below 5 percent. Despite the fact that at least a third of the Psalms are in a minor key, it seems that "the American church avoids lament."[6]

Now I don't mean to lay the blame solely on worship pastors and musicians. The absence of lament is not entirely their fault. But as I've talked with our worship leaders about this, we've wondered together what it would look like to recapture the balance of the Psalms in the songs we write today. I'm not arguing for one out of every three songs, but I do hope that some creative musicians will take up this challenge to bring balance to our corporate worship diet. We need good, substantive songs of lament.

---

5. Soong-Chan Rah, *Prophetic Lament: A Call for Justice in Troubled Times* (Downers Grove: InterVarsity Press, 2015), 22.

6. Rah, *Prophetic Lament*, 22.

My guess, however, is that contemporary songs of lament may not be sung frequently until the American church feels the full weight of our exile. But maybe we could start writing songs with lament themes so when dark clouds loom, we'll know there is a different tune to be sung. In the same way that Negro spirituals reflected the suffering of our black brothers and sisters generations ago, so too our "positive and encouraging" diet probably reflects the spirit of our cultural Christianity today. A slight adjustment would be helpful.

My point is simply that celebration is not the only song we should sing. There are other important genres for us to learn. More people than we probably know are weeping in our Sunday celebrations. Worship leaders and songwriters might be able to welcome them by singing a few of their songs. Or at least it would be wise to try.

Small Groups

Among the most practical places for lament to be applied are the smaller gatherings of God's people. Whether small groups, women's Bible studies, Sunday school classes, or accountability groups, there will be numerous opportunities for people to join together as the pains and challenges of life unfold. Lament can be a language that brings comfort to the hurting and a way for the group to help.

Unfortunately, I've seen groups stumble their way through the grief of others. For example, during prayer-request time in a small group, a couple shares a painful issue they are walking through. Their candid, heartfelt pain creates an awkward heaviness. What should happen next? How do you prevent Jim from offering his well-meaning but shallow advice on how to fix the issue? Do you simply move on to take the next request? How do you really care for hurting people if they open up?

I think the answer is lament. Imagine what would happen if the leader seized the moment, opened up a lament psalm, and invited the group to echo the words of the psalmist on behalf of their friends. Consider the kind of grace that could be applied as brothers and sisters in Christ entered into one another's pain, while collectively carrying their sorrow to the Lord.

A man in our church named Glen knows this kind of healing grace. He is a young widower with four kids under the age of fourteen. He and his wife, Nancy, faithfully served with Cru (Campus Crusade for Christ) for over two decades. They loved sharing Christ with college students and discipling them.

However, Nancy was diagnosed with a high-grade neuro-endocrine tumor, an aggressive and rare form of cancer. Over eleven months, she battled through chemotherapy. For a while, it looked like the cancer might be in remission. But sadly, it returned with a vengeance. Her cancer was terminal. With this grave diagnosis, Glen and Nancy invited their small group to lament with them as her health declined. Their small group walked the valley with them.

Their group met every other week for their normal study of the Scriptures, but they would always make time to grieve with Glen and Nancy. The group would listen to Nancy share as she walked through the spiritual struggles that a terminal diagnosis brings. They rejoiced with her as opportunities for evangelism emerged, or as she reached out to people with whom she desired reconciliation. They wept with Glen as he talked about his fears of being alone and raising four kids. They groaned together as Nancy's physical appearance noticeably changed near the end. Through countless prayer times, they would grieve the valley Glen and Nancy were walking through. This band of believers came alongside them and entered their pain. They lamented together.

A few months before Nancy passed away, I met with Glen, Nancy, and their small group. We talked about their journey together, and what it meant for Glen and Nancy to have close friends enter their pain. The beauty and strength I observed that night provided yet another example of the power and value of lament. Glen and Nancy were hurting and scared of the unknown before them. But they were finding a pathway to trust the Lord and his Word. Lamenting together in their small group was key. By prayerfully pouring out their sorrows and their hopes to the Lord together, not retreating or silencing the struggle, they found strength, hope, and mercy in the dark clouds of cancer.

As we think about where lament could be practiced, intimate or small gatherings of believers should top our list. Imagine what would happen if small group leaders, elders, women's Bible study leaders, and youth ministry volunteers were fluent in the language of lament. I've observed, firsthand, the power of this prayer language.

"Community" in the church should mean lamenting together.

Racial Issues

I've saved the issue of race for the end because it may be one of the most relevant and complicated applications of lament in our contemporary church culture. Lament has the potential to provide a first step toward uniting people when hurt and misunderstanding are in the air. The sacred song of sorrow does not resolve all racial tension or injustice. But it does give the church a prayer language of compassion and a starting point toward understanding.

I'm writing this chapter on the heels of a series of high-profile, racial incidents. A group of white supremacists marched to a Confederate statue in the center of a city in Virginia. The news media carried images of torch-carrying white men shouting, "You will not replace us!" and "White Lives Matter." Along with this, there were protests in another state after a judge issued a not-guilty judgment in a trial of a former police officer accused of shooting a black man at the conclusion of a high-speed chase. At issue was whether the man was in possession of a gun or if the officer planted a weapon after the shooting. While television commentators debated the merits of the case, the streets were filled with angry protestors.

How should the church respond to moments like this?

The issues are so complicated and the pain so raw. My response in the past has been to err on the side of silence because I don't know what to say. That was the reason my brother Jermaine asked me about Ferguson.

But my pastoral silence sent the wrong message.

This is where I think corporate lament can be uniquely helpful. For those of us who have not experienced pain or unfair treatment because of our ethnicity, lament can be the language we use to weep with those who weep (Rom. 12:15). It allows our first voice—our first step—to be one of compassion. We can turn to God in prayer and join our minority brothers and sisters in their pain. We can identify the brokenness in our world, mourn the racial tensions that still exist, and offer our "complaint" to God about the history of injustice, misunderstanding, and racism. Together we can ask God for healing and for kindness in our hearts. Rather than allowing racial tension to drive a wedge between us or to frighten us into silence, lament can invite all of us on a journey toward seeking God's grace together.

Lament can also be the place for the expression of fear and hurt for our minority brothers and sisters. When national events resurface personal pain and shine a light on potential injustice or inequity, lament offers a redemptive framework as people are led to turn, complain, ask, and trust. Lament invites those who have been hurt by mistreatment to turn to the author of all healing. Through complaint they are able to bluntly share their pain. In asking for God's help, they're able to clarify for themselves and others what their heart longs for. And by ending with trust, people struggling with the lingering pain of racism can reaffirm their hope in the One who judges justly (1 Pet. 2:23).

Lament provides the tracks along which the pain of racial issues can move forward.

Don't misunderstand me. I'm not naive enough to believe that lament is the single solution for racial tension. There is much work to be done in listening, understanding, addressing injustice, and fostering hope. But I do think lament is a starting point—a place where people from majority and minority backgrounds can meet. The beauty of this biblical language of sorrow is its ability to provide a bridge robust enough to handle outrage and empathy, frustration and faith, fear and hope. Lament can be our first step toward one another when racial tension could drive a wedge.

It is a God-given means for vocalizing complicated and loaded pain.

For centuries lament has been the minor-key voice of people in pain. It is the language of loss that should be prayed together. While lament can be applied to moments of individual loss, its redemptive power is multiplied as we pursue it together. Whether it is expressed in a funeral, modeled in a sermon, prayed or sung in a worship service, applied in a small group, or voiced in the middle of racial tension, lamenting together is an essential ministry of the body of Christ.

There is a song of mercy to be sung under dark clouds. The church should lead the way. Through every injustice and every sorrow, followers of Jesus can help one another find their way through the pain.

Lament is the language of loss as we grieve together.

Reflection Questions

1. Describe a time when you missed an opportunity to lament with someone because you were unaware of the pain or didn't know what to say? Looking back, what lessons have you learned.

2. Why do you think funerals are often more about celebration than about sorrow? How have you observed this balance or lack of balance?

3. What are some creative ways lament might be appropriately applied in your Sunday worship services? What challenges might stand in the way of this happening?

4. How could your small group, Bible study, or Sunday school class practice lament more effectively?

5. Have you experienced or witnessed a positive experience with lament in a group setting? Describe what transpired and why it was helpful?

6. When considering racial tension, how has this chapter helped you see the role of lament in bringing different ethnicities together? How could lament start a healing process or a conversation?

7. How does lament uniquely serve people in a majority culture or a minority culture? What role should it play in each group?

Conclusion

Dark Clouds, Deep Mercy

The Journey Ahead

The clouds ye so much dread
Are big with mercy. . . .
William Cowper

My journey in learning to lament began with "No, Lord! Please not this." But thankfully—in God's grace—it didn't end there. The avalanche of pain unearthed the question *why*. Over time I learned the hope of resting in *who* God is. Discovering the grace of lament was part of this pilgrimage. I hope you are on the same journey.

Lament is the song we sing in the space between pain and promise. It becomes the path between the poles of a hard life and trusting God's goodness. Lament helps us embrace two truths at the same time: hard is hard; hard is not bad.

The historic minor key of lament gives us permission to vocalize our pain while moving us toward God-centered worship. It is an act of faith as we turn to God, lay out our complaints, ask God to keep his promises, and reaffirm our trust in him. Lament is more than tears and crying. To cry is human. But to lament is Christian.

It is how we tunnel our way to hope.[1]

Lament not only gives voice to our struggles. By entering into it, we also discover there are lessons to be learned. Lament tunes our heart to truths undergirding our lives and the world in which we live. This liturgy of loss expands our view beyond our personal struggles and painful experiences. It invites us to ponder the brokenness of life, the source of hope, the problem of misplaced trust, and even the role of Christians as guides through the darkness of grief.

Lament is how we tunnel our way to truth.

Mercy in Dark Clouds

The aim of this book has been to help you discover the grace of lament. When dark clouds roll in, lament is the path to find mercy—even as the clouds linger. Lament is the bridge between dark clouds and deep mercy.

As I said in the introduction, the title of this book is taken from two verses in Lamentations that seem to be contradictory.

> How the Lord in his anger
>   has set the daughter of Zion under a cloud!
>   (Lam. 2:1)

> The steadfast love of the LORD never ceases,
>   his mercies never come to an end. (Lam. 3:22)

---

1. Jeff Medders, "Vocalizing and Velocity" (sermon presented in the series Learning to Lament, Redeemer Church, Tomball, TX, June 11, 2017), http://www.makingmuch ofjesus.org/sermons/sermon/2017-06-11/vocalizing-velocity.

Our journey has shown us that this paradox is central to the hope of lament. It is the prayer language that stakes its claim on the promises of God in the pains of life. Dark clouds may come, but divine mercy never ends.

Lament is how we experience grace no matter what we face.

Forsaken Yet Not Despised

We've learned that trusting in God and deep sorrow are not mutually exclusive. They coexist in the lament journey. Pouring out one's heart—even in blunt complaint—leads to hope and assurance. The Psalms are filled with this spiritual posture.

A few verses from Psalm 22 make this clear:

> My God, my God, why have you forsaken me?
>> Why are you so far from saving me, from the words of
>>> my groaning? . . .
>
> For he has not despised or abhorred
>> the affliction of the afflicted,
> and he has not hidden his face from him,
>> but has heard, when he cried to him. . . .
>
> The afflicted shall eat and be satisfied;
>> those who seek him shall praise the LORD!
>> May your hearts live forever! (vv. 1, 24, 26).

As we learned in chapter 3, this psalm was famously quoted by Jesus on the cross. It was his prayerful complaint in the final moments of his earthly life. But we also know that he was not forsaken forever. The lament of Good Friday was answered three days later with the empty tomb. The greatest injustice in history became the greatest display of divine mercy. Tragedy became triumph. Lament was the voice in between.

J. R. R. Tolkien is the famous author of *The Hobbit* and *The Lord of the Rings*. According to Skye Jethani in his book *With: Reimagining the Way You Relate to God*, Tolkien frequently wrote storylines that featured eucatastrophe.[2] If you've never heard this word before, it's for good reason. Tolkien made it up. He created the word as a way of combining something bad (*catastrophe*) with something good (*eu*). A catastrophe is an unexpected evil, and by adding *eu* as a prefix, he expresses the unexpected appearance of goodness.[3] If you've read Tolkien or seen the films, you can probably think of numerous examples where eucatastrophe is a critical part of the story. Tolkien describes this moment as "the sudden happy turn in a story which pierces you with a joy that brings you to tears . . . because it is a sudden glimpse of Truth."[4]

Lament is the language that helps you believe catastrophe can become eucatastrophe. It vocalizes the pain of the moment while believing that help is on the way.

Lament gives us hope because it gives us a glimpse of truth.

How Long? Until . . .

Lament is the language of waiting for God's justice to be accomplished. Through the Psalms and Lamentations we've learned that lament is the way we live with pain beyond belief and divine sovereignty beyond comprehension. Revelation 6 records the heartfelt cry for justice by those "who had been slain for the word of God and for the witness they had borne" (v. 9). Their lament should sound familiar by now: "They cried out with a

---

2. Skye Jethani, *With: Reimagining the Way You Relate to God* (Nashville: Thomas Nelson, 2011), 99.
3. Jethani, *With*, 99.
4. J. R. R. Tolkien, *The Letters of J. R. R. Tolkien*, ed. Humphrey Carpenter (Boston: Houghton Mifflin, 1981), 100.

loud voice, 'O Sovereign Lord, holy and true, how long before you will judge and avenge our blood on those who dwell on the earth?'" (v. 10). The answer to their complaint is the gift of a white robe, symbolizing purity and a somber instruction: "Then they were each given a white robe and told to rest a little longer, until the number of their fellow servants and their brothers should be complete, who were to be killed as they themselves had been" (v. 11). While the martyrs wait for God's purposes to unfold and for justice to be done, they lament. Divine resolution will come (see vv. 15–17). However, waiting—even "resting"— is part of the plan.

Lament vocalizes a desire for justice that is unfulfilled.

Lament Will Not Be Forever

Finally, we've seen that Christians lament expectantly. Knowing God's goodness and believing in his sovereignty cause us to pray for divine intervention to the painful paradoxes of life. We know the brokenness of sin that causes all lament. And we believe the death and resurrection of Jesus inaugurated the defeat of sin, death, and all tears. In our sorrow, we long for the day when lament will be no more: "He will wipe away every tear from their eyes, and death shall be no more, neither shall there be mourning, nor crying, nor pain anymore, for the former things have passed away" (Rev. 21:4).

One of the greatest joys of the new heavens and the new earth will be the absence of all songs of sorrow. Perhaps we'll sing the Psalms, but we'll not sing all of them. In God's presence there will be no need to lament. All our complaints will be complete. Our requests will have been answered. Praise will be in the air we breathe.

Heavenly praise will replace our earthly groaning.

I can hardly wait. You too?

The Journey Ahead

Until that day we live between two worlds. Believers in Jesus are called to walk the path between earthly brokenness and heavenly restoration.

Lament is our song for this journey.

You may need lament because your valley experience is happening right now. As you walk this dark road, allow lament to do its work in your life. Keep talking to God. Don't quit. Lay out your complaints. Ask boldly for what you need, and make the choice to trust—every day. Let your pain become a platform for praise. But don't stop there! Let lament become your teacher and a new way to see the world. Let it guide you into mercies yet unknown.

For others, dark clouds are coming in the not-so-distant future. If you live long enough, you will have seasons of sorrow. I guarantee it. Rather than live in a resigned state of despair or worry, you can learn the grace of lament before the storm rages. Embracing this divinely given language will not only deepen your understanding of God's grace; it will prepare you to navigate life when "sorrows like sea billows roll."[5] But it can also equip you for something more.

You see, Christianity needs competent lamenters. The gospel empowers the followers of Jesus to enter the dark moments of people's lives. Those who know the story of hope and who believe in God's goodness can be conduits of his grace. Lament allows us to hear the brokenness around us, weep with those who weep, and walk with them on the long road of sorrow.

No matter where we are in our journey, lament is a means of mercy.

Lament is how you move from *no* to *yes*, and from *why* to *who*. While hard is hard, hard is not bad, because lament helps us embrace this paradox. And it changes us along the way.

---

5. From Horatio Spafford, "It Is Well with My Soul" (1873).

A little girl I never knew started a lifelong journey in lament. A stillborn daughter broke my heart but gave me new eyes to see the world. Lament became my life and a means of grace to my soul. It opened my heart to lessons I never expected. It drew me into depths of worship I never knew existed. That's my journey. And wherever you are in yours, I invite you: keep lamenting.

In dark clouds there is deep mercy as we discover the grace of lament.

Reflection Questions

1. What prompted you to start reading this book? What questions were you originally trying to answer?
2. How has your understanding of lament changed by reading this book? What new insights have you gained?
3. How has your understanding of God and your love for him grown by considering this subject?
4. What questions still remain unanswered for you when it comes to lament?
5. As you look toward the journey ahead, list the three most important truths that you need to remember for the next year.
6. How can you now help other people who are walking through a dark valley? What action steps do you need to take?
7. Take a few moments and write out a prayer of gratitude to God for what you've learned. You may want to write it in the back of this book. Let that prayer become a memorial for your journey ahead.

Twenty Complaints

Laments contain various complaints expressing struggle, questions, outrage, and frustration. The following passages are examples of the unique complaints found in the psalms of lament:

Why?

Why, O LORD, do you stand far away?
  Why do you hide yourself in times of trouble? (Ps. 10:1)

Why does the wicked renounce God
  and say in his heart, "You will not call to account"?
    (Ps. 10:13)

My God, my God, why have you forsaken me?
  Why are you so far from saving me, from the words of
    my groaning? (Ps. 22:1)

I say to God, my rock:
  "Why have you forgotten me?
Why do I go mourning
  because of the oppression of the enemy?" (Ps. 42:9)

For you are the God in whom I take refuge;
  why have you rejected me?
Why do I go about mourning
  because of the oppression of the enemy? (Ps. 43:2)

Awake! Why are you sleeping, O Lord?
  Rouse yourself! Do not reject us forever! (Ps. 44:23)

O God, why do you cast us off forever?
  Why does your anger smoke against the sheep of your
    pasture? (Ps. 74:1)

Why do you hold back your hand, your right hand?
  Take it from the fold of your garment and destroy
    them! (Ps. 74:11)

Why then have you broken down its walls,
  so that all who pass along the way pluck its fruit?
    (Ps. 80:12)

O LORD, why do you cast my soul away?
  Why do you hide your face from me? (Ps. 88:14)

How?

O LORD, how many are my foes!
  Many are rising against me. (Ps. 3:1)

How long, O Lord, will you look on?
  Rescue me from their destruction,
  my precious life from the lions! (Ps. 35:17)

How long, O God, is the foe to scoff?
  Is the enemy to revile your name forever? (Ps. 74:10)

Remember this, O LORD, how the enemy scoffs,
  and a foolish people reviles your name. (Ps. 74:18)

Arise, O God, defend your cause;
> remember how the foolish scoff at you all the day!
>> (Ps. 74:22)

O Lᴏʀᴅ God of hosts,
> how long will you be angry with your people's
>> prayers? (Ps. 80:4)

How long, O Lᴏʀᴅ? Will you hide yourself forever?
> How long will your wrath burn like fire? (Ps. 89:46)

Return, O Lᴏʀᴅ! How long?
> Have pity on your servants! (Ps. 90:13)

O Lᴏʀᴅ, how long shall the wicked,
> how long shall the wicked exult? (Ps. 94:3)

How shall we sing the Lᴏʀᴅ's song
> in a foreign land? (Ps. 137:4)

Appendix 2

Psalms of Lament

Personal An individual vocalizing pain, grief, fear, or some other strong emotion	3, 4, 5, 7, 10, 13, 17, 22, 25, 26, 28, 31, 39, 42, 43, 54, 55, 56, 57, 59, 61, 64, 70, 71, 77, 86, 120, 141, 142
Corporate A group or nation vocalizing pain, grief, fear, or some other strong emotion	12, 44, 58, 60, 74, 79, 80, 83, 85, 90, 94, 123, 126
Repentant An individual or group expressing regret or sorrow for sin	6, 32, 38, 51, 102, 130, 143
Imprecatory An individual or group expressing outrage and a strong desire for justice	35, 69, 83, 88, 109, 137, 140
Partial Sections of lament within other psalms	9:13–20; 27:7–14; 40:11–17
Debatable Psalms that some consider to be lament in total or in part	14, 36, 41, 52, 53, 63, 78, 81, 89, 106, 125, 129, 139*

* Rosann Catalano, "How Long, O Lord? A Systematic Study of the Theology and Practice of Biblical Lament" (doctoral diss., Toronto School of Theology, 1988), 59; Dennis Bratcher, "Types of Psalms," Christian Resource Institute: The Voice, accessed January 30, 2018, http://www.crivoice.org/psalmtypes.html.

Appendix 3

Learning-to-Lament Worksheet

Movements of Lament	Psalm ___	My Lament
Turn to God Address God as you come to him in prayer. This is sometimes combined with complaint.		
Bring Your Complaint Identify in blunt language the specific pain or injustice. *Why* or *how* is often part of the complaint.		
Ask Boldly Specifically call upon God to act in a manner that fits his character and resolves your complaint.		
Choose to Trust Affirm God's worthiness to be trusted, and commit to praising him.		

Learning to Lament Worksheet, Sample 1

Movements of Lament	Psalm 86	My Lament
Turn to God Address God as you come to him in prayer. This is sometimes combined with complaint.	v. 1: "Incline your ear, O Lord, and answer me, / for I am poor and needy." v. 6: "Give ear, O Lord, to my prayer; / listen to my plea for grace."	God, I need you to hear me. I'm hurting and in pain. I'm asking for you to listen to my lament. I desperately need your grace today.
Bring Your Complaint Identify in blunt language the specific pain or injustice. *Why* or *how* is often part of the complaint.	v. 14: "O God, insolent men have risen up against me; / a band of ruthless men seeks my life, / and they do not set you before them."	You've heard every unfair word, and you know how I've been misunderstood. I'm upset. I'm defensive. I want to strike back with more words. I don't feel like they care. It doesn't end. I don't know what to do.

Movements of Lament	Psalm 86	My Lament
Ask Boldly Specifically call upon God to act in a manner that fits his character and resolves your complaint.	v. 2: "Preserve my life . . . / save your servant." v. 3: "Be gracious to me, O Lord." v. 11: "Teach me your way, O LORD . . . / unite my heart to fear your name." v. 16: "Turn to me and be gracious to me; / give your strength to your servant." v. 17: "Show me a sign of your favor."	Teach me every lesson you want me to learn through this. Help me know what to say or not to say. Make my heart love your purposes more than I love my reputation. Help me know that you are listening and that you care for me. I need help, God. My heart is so divided. One minute I think good thoughts. The next, ugly thoughts. Pour out your grace on me, please!
Choose to Trust Affirm God's worthiness to be trusted, and commit to praising him.	v. 8: "There is none like you among the gods, O Lord." v. 12: "I give thanks to you, O Lord my God, with my whole heart." v. 13: "Great is your steadfast love." v. 15: "But you, O Lord, are a God merciful and gracious, / slow to anger and abounding in steadfast love and faithfulness" v. 17: "You, LORD, have helped me and comforted me."	None of this is a surprise to you. You've heard every word. You know what I'm feeling, and you are greater than anything I face. You can supply what I need and give me the strength if others don't understand. I can trust you with what people say about me. You've helped me through many worse situations. So I'm going to keep my eyes on you. I'm trusting you. I'm still going to worship you. Thank you.

Learning to Lament Worksheet, Sample 2

Movements of Lament	Psalm 3	My Lament
Turn to God Address God as you come to him in prayer. This is sometimes combined with complaint.	v. 1: "O LORD, how many are my foes!"	Father, here I am again with a heart full of worries and fears. I'm praying to you by faith with a heart that is struggling.
Bring Your Complaint Identify in blunt language the specific pain or injustice. *Why* or *how* is often part of the complaint.	v. 1: "Many are rising against me." v. 2: "Many are saying of my soul, / 'There is no salvation for him in God.'"	I'm totally over-whelmed, God! The pressures of life, family, and ministry feel too great. I don't have enough energy, strength, or wisdom for all the challenges. I'm drowning. And it gives rise to unbelief in my heart. I start to doubt your faithfulness to me.

Movements of Lament	Psalm 3	My Lament
Ask Boldly Specifically call upon God to act in a manner that fits his character and resolves your complaint.	v. 7: "Arise, O LORD! / Save me, O my God! / For you strike all my enemies on the cheek; / you break the teeth of the wicked." v. 8: "Salvation belongs to the LORD; / [may] your blessing be on your people!"	Help me God! Right now. I'm writing this prayer because I need you to reorient my thinking. Conquer the lies of the enemy that run through my mind. Grant me the ability to trust you. Please, do it now! Bless me today, please God. Help me know you are with me.
Choose to Trust Affirm God's worthiness to be trusted, and commit to praising him.	v. 3: "But you, O LORD, are a shield about me, / my glory, and the lifter of my head." v. 4: "I cried aloud to the LORD, / and he answered me from his holy hill." v. 5: "I lay down and slept; / I woke again for the LORD sustained me." v. 6: "I will not be afraid of many thousands of people / who have set themselves against me all around."	But God—yes! You are a shield for me. Even now you are protecting me and helping me through the gospel of Christ and the Holy Spirit. You've never failed me. Every day your mercies have been new to me. You've given me every reason to trust you. So I'm not going to give in to fear today. I'm going to walk by faith today in your ability to help me. Here we go!

Appendix 4

But, Yet, And

A turning point in a lament psalm is marked by the word *but*, *yet*, or *and*. This is the movement from complaint to asking boldly and/or choosing to trust. In some cases, the specific word is not present, but the tone of the sentence fits the purpose. Some examples are listed in the following chart.

Description	Passages*
Personal Reflections	"But I am like a deaf man" (Ps. 38:13). "But I am poor and needy" (Ps. 70:5). "But as for me, I shall walk in my integrity" (Ps. 26:11). "But as for me, my prayer is to you" (Ps. 69:13). "But I call to God" (Ps. 55:16).
Requests to God	"But you, O LORD—how long?" (Ps. 6:3). "But you, O LORD, do not be far off!" (Ps. 22:19). "You, LORD God of hosts. . . . / Rouse yourself" (Ps. 59:5).
Statements of Trust	"But I have trusted in your steadfast love" (Ps. 13:5). "But I trust in you" (Ps. 31:14). "But I am like a green olive tree. . . . / I trust in the steadfast love of God" (Ps. 52:8). "Then my soul will rejoice in the LORD" (Ps. 35:9). "But I will hope continually" (Ps. 71:14). "Behold, God is my helper" (Ps. 54:4).
Statements of Praise	"Yet you are holy" (Ps. 22:3). "But you, O LORD, are enthroned forever" (Ps. 102:12). "But you will remain. / . . . you are the same" (Ps. 102:26–27). "But you, O Lord, are a God merciful and gracious" (Ps. 86:15). "But you, O LORD, are a shield" (Ps. 3:3). "But you, O God, will cast them down" (Ps. 55:23). "But you, O LORD, laugh at them" (Ps. 59:8). "Let them curse, but you will bless" (Ps. 109:28). "But God shoots his arrow at them" (Ps. 64:7).

* Adapted from Claus Westermann, *Praise and Lament in the Psalms* (Atlanta: John Knox, 1981), 70–71.

Bibliography

Billings, Todd. *Rejoicing in Lament: Wrestling with Incurable Cancer and Life in Christ.* Grand Rapids, MI: Brazos, 2015.

Boice, James Montgomery. *Psalms*, vol. 2, *Psalms 42–106.* An Expositional Commentary. Grand Rapids, MI: Baker, 2005.

Bowling, Andrew. "1071 לֵבָב." In *Theological Wordbook of the Old Testament*, edited by R. Laird Harris, Gleason L. Archer Jr., and Bruce K. Waltke, 466. Chicago: Moody Press, 1999.

Bratcher, Dennis. "Types of Psalms." Christian Resource Institute: The Voice. Accessed January 30, 2018. http://www.crivoice.org /psalmtypes.html.

Brauns, Chris. *Unpacking Forgiveness: Biblical Answers for Complex Questions and Deep Wounds.* Wheaton, IL: Crossway, 2008.

Brown, Francis, Samuel Rolles Driver, and Charles Augustus Briggs. *Enhanced Brown-Driver-Briggs Hebrew and English Lexicon.* Oxford: Clarendon, 1977.

Card, Michael. *A Sacred Sorrow: Reaching Out to God in the Lost Language of Lament.* Colorado Springs: NavPress, 2005.

Catalano, Rosann. "How Long, O Lord? A Systematic Study of the Theology and Practice of Biblical Lament." Doctoral diss., Toronto School of Theology, 1988.

Eklund, Rebekah Ann. "Lord, Teach Us How to Grieve: Jesus' Laments and Christian Hope." ThD diss., Duke Divinity School, 2012.

Fleece, Esther. *No More Faking Fine: Ending the Pretending.* Grand Rapids, MI: Zondervan, 2017.

Garrett, Duane, and Paul R. House. *Song of Songs/Lamentations.* Word Biblical Commentary. Dallas: Word, 2004.

Gleddiesmith, Stacey. "My God, My God, Why? Understanding the Lament Psalms." *Reformed Worship*, June 2010. www.reformedworship.org/article/june-2010/my-god-my-god-why.

Harrison, R. K. *Jeremiah and Lamentations: An Introduction and Commentary.* Tyndale Old Testament Commentaries. Downers Grove, IL: InterVarsity Press, 1973.

Huey, F. B. *Jeremiah, Lamentations.* The New American Commentary. Nashville: Broadman & Holman, 1993.

Jethani, Skye. *With: Reimagining the Way You Relate to God.* Nashville: Thomas Nelson, 2011.

Jinkins, Michael. *In the House of the Lord: Inhabiting the Psalms of Lament.* Collegeville, MN: Liturgical, 1989.

Keller, Timothy. *Counterfeit Gods: The Empty Promises of Money, Sex, and Power, and the Only Hope That Matters.* New York: Dutton, 2009.

———. *Walking with God through Pain and Suffering.* New York: Riverhead, 2013.

Lewis, C. S. *The Problem of Pain.* New York: Collier, 1962.

Medders, Jeff. "Vocalizing and Velocity." Sermon presented in the series Learning to Lament, Redeemer Church, Tomball, TX, June 11, 2017. http://www.makingmuchofjesus.org/sermons/sermon/2017-06-11/vocalizing-velocity.

Mohler, Albert. "Aftermath: Lessons from the 2012 Election." Albert Mohler (blog), November 7, 2012. www.albertmohler.com/2012/11/07/aftermath-lessons-from-the-2012-election.

Piper, John. *The Hidden Smile of God: The Fruit of Affliction in the Lives of John Bunyan, William Cowper, and David Brainerd.* Wheaton, IL: Crossway, 2001.

Protestant Episcopal Church. "The Order for the Administration of the Lord's Supper." In the Book of Common Prayer (1928).

Accessed January 27, 2018. http://justus.anglican.org/resources /bcp/1928/HC.htm.

Rah, Soong-Chan. *Prophetic Lament: A Call for Justice in Troubled Times*. Downers Grove, IL: InterVarsity Press, 2015.

Smith, Steven W. *Recapturing the Voice of God: Shaping Sermons Like Scripture*. Nashville: B&H Academic, 2015.

Stebbing, H. *The Complete Poetical Works of William Cowper*. New York: D. Appleton, 1869.

Swanson, James. *Dictionary of Biblical Languages with Semantic Domains: Hebrew (Old Testament)*. Oak Harbor, IL: Logos Research Systems, 1997.

Tolkien, J. R. R. *The Letters of J. R. R. Tolkien*. Edited by Humphrey Carpenter. Boston: Houghton Mifflin, 1981.

Waltke, Bruce K., James M. Houston, and Erika Moore. *The Psalms as Christian Lament: A Historical Commentary*. Grand Rapids, MI: Eerdmans, 2014.

Westermann, Claus. *Praise and Lament in the Psalms*. Atlanta: John Knox, 1981.

Wills, Amanda, Sara Sidner, and Mallory Simon. "Why Charlotte Exploded and Tulsa Prayed." CNN, September 22, 2016. www .cnn.com/2016/09/22/us/tulsa-charlotte-shooting-protests/index .html.

Witherall, Gary. *Total Abandon*. With Elizabeth Newenhuyse. Carol Stream, IL: Tyndale, 2005.

Wolterstorff, Nicolas. *Lament for a Son*. Grand Rapids, MI: Eerdmans, 1987.

Woollard, Neal. "Why We Added a Prayer of Lament to Our Sunday Gathering." 9Marks (website), June 20, 2018. https://www .9marks.org/article/why-we-added-a-prayer-of-lament-to-our -sunday-gathering/.

———. "What Does a Prayer of Lament Sound Like?" 9Marks (website), June 25, 2018. https://www.9marks.org/article/what -does-a-prayer-of-lament-sound-like/.

General Index

Jinkins, Michael, 48, 76, 78
Job, 82
justice, unfulfilled, 193

"keep trusting the One who keeps you
    trusting," 85, 171–72
Keller, Timothy, 105, 111, 124
Kinkade, Thomas, 105

lament
    affirms God's sovereignty, 147–48
    awakens the soul, 103–4
    as category for complaint, 159
    as Christian, 26, 38, 190
    definition of, 28
    diversity of, 61
    as expansive prayer language, 65
    expresses the gospel through tears,
        36–37
    as framework for feeling, 159
    as gift from God, 19
    and hope, 28, 29, 110, 119
    as language for loss, 159
    leads to Christ, 150–52
    leads to rejoicing, 81
    leads to trust, 28, 83, 158
    as memorial, 90, 152
    not a simplistic formula, 33
    as path to praise, 28
    pivots on God's promises, 85
    as process for pain, 160
    requires faith, 31–34
    as road map to grace, 140–42, 144,
        146
    as solution for silence, 159
    as song for journey, 194
    as teacher, 152
    as transformative, 106
    and turning to God, 129
    unfamiliarity with, 18–19
    as way to worship, 160
    will not be forever, 193
Lamentations (book), 90–91
    background of, 92–94
    ending of, 139
    honesty of, 108

on idols, 123–25
    wisdom of, 100–104
    written to exiles, 123
leadership failures, 132–34
learning from lament, 22, 89, 158, 165
learning to lament, 15, 22, 158, 165
learning-to-lament worksheet, 203–7
"let justice be done," 62
Lewis, C. S., 89
living with lament, 22, 158, 165
loneliness, 169–70

Maclaren, Alexander, 32
man of sorrows, 66
mercy of God
    and brokenness, 20–21, 28
    never ends, 112–14
miscarriages, 18
Mohler, Al, 122
money, 126

new covenant, 150
new heavens and new earth, 193
New Jerusalem, 99
now and not yet, 74

oppression, 50
Owens, Ray, 145

pain
    awakens the need of God, 60
    as God's megaphone to rouse a deaf
        world, 89–90
Paul, lament of, 161
personal laments, 201
Piper, John, 85, 171
praying the Bible, 52–53
praying the gospel, 36–37
preaching on lament, 180–81
prodigal children, 67–68
prosperity, 30
providence, 115
psalms of lament, 29–30, 43, 83, 167,
    201
    boldness in, 61–65
    complaints in, 197–99

Scripture Index

A Companion Devotional Journal to *Dark Clouds, Deep Mercy*

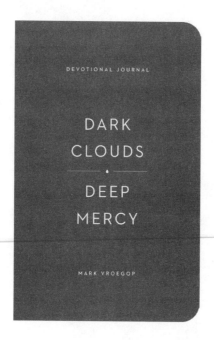

This companion journal is ideal for applying the knowledge you gained about lament in *Dark Clouds, Deep Mercy* and practicing it in your own life. Each of the fifteen devotions is focused on one psalm of lament and includes an inspirational overview, a quote from the book, space to write a personal lament, four reflection questions, and a brief prayer.

For more information, visit **crossway.org**.